FAST TRACK
YOUR
CALLING

**HOW TO FUEL YOUR DRIVE
WITH EVERY ASSIGNMENT**

GERREN A. SPRAUVE

Fast-Track Your Calling: How To Fuel Your Drive With Every Assignment **Copyright © 2019 by Gerren Sprauve**

All rights reserved. No part of this book may be reproduced in any form or by any means—electronic, mechanical, photocopying, scanning or otherwise—without written permission from the author, except by a reviewer who may quote.

ISBN: 9781093485080

Imprint: Independently published

Printed in the United States of America

This publication is designed to provide accurate and authoritative information with regard to the subject matter covered. It is sold with the understanding that neither the author nor publisher is engaged in rendering legal, accounting, or other professional advice. If legal advice or other expert assistance is required, the services of a competent professional person should be sought.

What's Next?

www.GerrenSprauve.com/Assessment

What is your calling? How do you know if what you are doing in life is what you should be doing? Is your calling closer than you think? This free assessment helps you get clarity on where you are supposed to be in your career, in your ministry, and in your life.

www.GerrenSprauve.com/Assessment

Contents

Dedication vi
Foreword 1
Chapter 1: I Found My Calling in a Toilet Bowl 5
Chapter 2: Why You (Still) Haven't Found Your Calling .. 41
Chapter 3: Closer Than You Think 59
Chapter 4: Self-Promotion Isn't Selfish 75
Chapter 5: It's Lonely Out Here 97
Chapter 6: You Have Arrived 115
Chapter 7: Fast Track for Everyone 135
Acknowledgments 163

Dedication

This book is dedicated to my amazing wife, Josie, who continues to support my journey as I deliver on the promises I made to her. That support allows me to be who I am to the people I meet.

This book is dedicated to my mother, who taught me how to learn, and to my father, who taught me how to serve.

Lastly, this book is dedicated to my guy—my coach—Eric Harmon. I wish you were here to experience "our next step."

Foreword

Gerren embraces an exuberance for life, and an acute, genuine interest in people, seldom found in today's world. Furthermore, he possesses the gift of helping others manifest their gifts, and reach their true goals.

Tired of being enslaved to the banality and tedium of the common job description, he broke off the shackles of the office cubicle that constrained his joie de vivre, and became a pioneer, blazing a trail of extraordinary service to people and organizations from myriad backgrounds and industries. He set a course for himself that most people never dream of...

He became the trusted advisors of executives, a brilliant public speaker, a motivating author, a compassionate helper of those in crisis, encourager of the lost, and inspirer of the hopeless. With the skill of a professional tight-rope walker, Gerren confidently traversed an aberrant high-wire, far above the nature of where most travel. Each step, carefully balancing, but deftly crossing cultural, socio-economic, racial, and political boundaries, to achieve his goal of taking people and organizations to exceptional heights and inconceivable destinations.

Like similar super-men of this genre, his Clark Kent-like, mild-mannered persona, has enabled people to not be intimidated by his superpowers of intuition, x-ray vision into their hearts, and strength to help them build a bridge to their dreams.

Armed with positivity, well-meaning inquisitiveness, and a few cleaning supplies, this soldier wore a uniform of few chevrons....a disarming, unassuming disguise...that of the janitor. If we haven't already, we will most likely wake up one day and ask....is this all there is? Most individuals will entertain the thought from time to time, bemoaning it inside...or aloud, but doing little more than perhaps treating the symptoms, but rarely administering a cure to the disease.

A physician of the soul, Gerren remedied his dis-ease, by restoring other's faith in themselves, by treating each person who has been fortunate enough to cross his path as a customer, brother, and friend.

If you are on the journey to becoming all that you can be, Gerren helps you to stop looking through the rear-view window of your life, and helps you to look through the windshield and focus on the road ahead. He provides a vehicle to get you where you want and need to go, based on your individual passions and talents, that the world so desperately needs.

—Shannon Faith Walsh

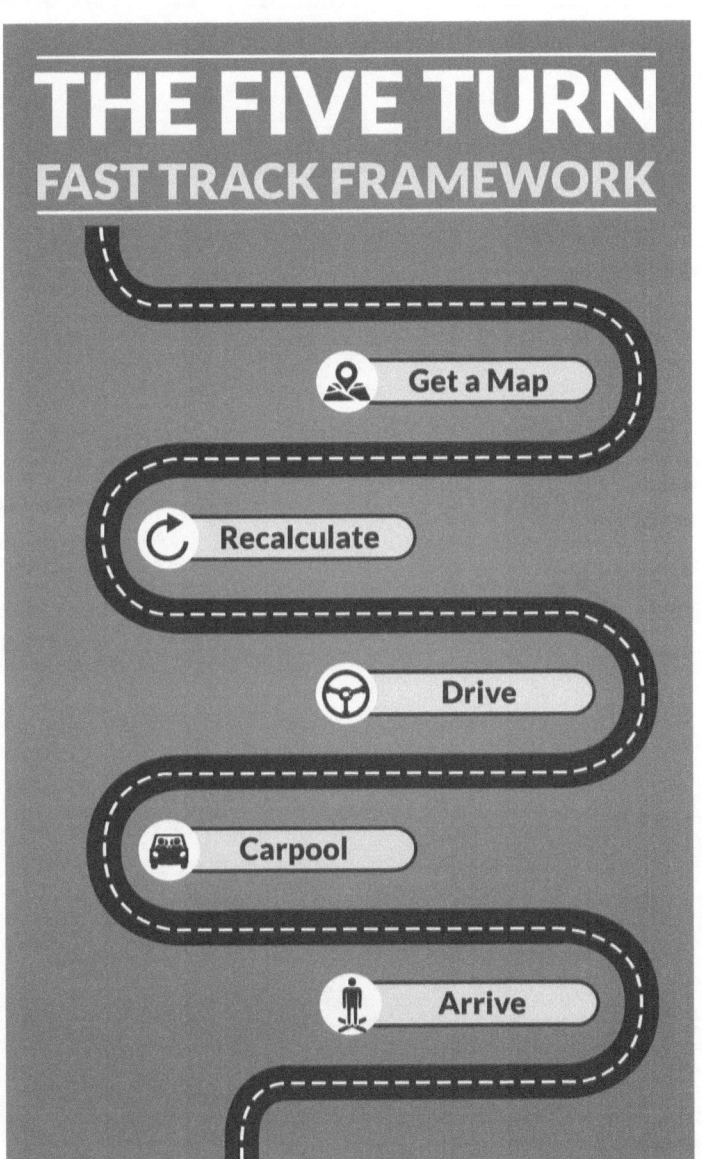

Chapter 1

I Found My Calling in a Toilet Bowl

Tap, tap, tap. Somebody was at my window. Voices crackled outside. A radio? I pulled my seat up, rubbed my eyes, and checked the door locks. *Locked. Okay, good.*

I'd been asleep since probably 1:00 a.m. here in the downtown Panera parking lot. Worked late. Not quite sunrise yet. Three hours of shut-eye. Not bad. Better than last night.

Tap, tap, tap, on my window. Harder this time. My body jumped. The face outside came into focus—no, two faces. Wait. *Three?* All white guys. In uniforms.

Ah, great. Here we go. Cops.

"What are you doing here, sir? And please step out of the vehicle," the officer said. "Keep your hands where we can see them."

I couldn't even see my hands, it was so dark out here. Should've parked closer to Panera. Radios crackled again. *Did he just call for more backup?* I dropped my half-empty bottle of Coca-Cola and—slowly—moved both hands to the steering wheel. All three officers had their hands on their holsters. *Be cool, Gerren, be cool. You haven't done anything wrong.*

"Good morning, officers," I said with a yawn. "I'm gonna unlock the door and come right out, okay?"

I took a quick look at the officer's badge—*Campbell.*

Officer Campbell nodded but put out a hand like he was telling oncoming traffic to stop. Confusing, to say the least.

I rolled down my tinted window the rest of the way and opened the door with my left hand. With my right, I reached into the cupholder and swiped a business card—the face of my company. Other than these cards and my cleaning equipment and solutions in the back seat, I had no other proof of my profession. *Work with what you have until you have what you need.*

"Gerren Sprauve." I stepped out of the vehicle. "I own a cleaning company. I have clients all over town. Here's my card. I'm just grabbing a nap and building up some energy before I hit the next job. I've cleaned three buildings already for the night. Got quite a few more to do before the weekend is up."

Officer Campbell's face changed. *He looks. . . impressed?* He took my card.

I Found My Calling in a Toilet Bowl

"Well, Mr. Sprauve, we didn't realize, uh . . ." He studied my card front and back. He checked for a logo on my polo—there was none—then scratched the back of his blond buzz cut.

"Oh, and Panera!" I broke the silence. "I do plan on giving them my business when they open." I pointed at the lit Panera sign. "I don't drink coffee. I just like their pastries. I figure sugar is healthier than straight-up caffeine shots. You know what I mean?" *Gotta build rapport quickly—or else.*

"Have you ever tasted their apple muffins?" the second officer piped up. "My kids love 'em."

Officer Campbell cleared his throat. "Good luck with those buildings this morning, Mr. Sprauve. How many buildings did you say? And it's just you?"

"Yup!" I shrugged. "One-man gang." Not the best word choice. "I mean, I clean all eleven buildings by myself, nonstop. I don't get to see my wife, Josie, much. But I promised her she wouldn't go hungry if she supported me going after this one dream. I feel that if I take good care of my clients now, I can build something amazing with this business. Then we can spend as much time together as we want."

"What's that hanging in the back of your car? You going to a funeral? Smells funny in here," the third cop said, peeking into my car with his flashlight. I didn't even see him get behind me.

I drove a 1998 white Nissan Maxima. Dark, soft, fabric interior. I'd traded a fresh vanilla fragrance for chemical odors. Solutions, mops, buckets, vacuums, and other equipment for scrubbing and waxing floors.

"Oh! My suit. You know, if a potential client calls me, I've got to be ready to meet with them. So I change out of the polo and jeans, put the suit on, go shake hands, and close the deal, if we're right for each other."

All three cops got quiet again. They stepped to their cruisers.

"You're okay, Mr. Sprauve." Officer Campbell waved back at me—and smiled. "We'll stick around till Panera opens. Nobody's going to bother you."

I waved back. I wiped my face on both sleeves. I was soaked in sweat, shaking all over. I stepped back to my car and let out a deep breath. I'd been holding it since they woke me up.

"Mr. Sprauve?" officer number three called out.

"Yes, sir?" I wheeled around.

"Get some rest, Mr. Sprauve."

"Will do. Thanks!"

"Coach, Psychologist, or Teacher"

A lot of people complain about not being happy at their jobs. It's not that the work itself is miserable. The problem is, the work is the *only* thing they're doing.

I Found My Calling in a Toilet Bowl

I used to be a claims adjuster at an insurance company, working mostly on workers' comp cases. I answered phones all day long, responding to attorneys and the occasional judge's office. I solved other people's problems so I could get employees back to work. It was . . . a lot of work. Our caseload was pretty overwhelming, and the environment, okay. It was a sea of cubicles, some taller than others. I got to speak to frustrated employers and employees who complained about their pay. I learned of many ways in which someone could get hurt on a job and many ways in which someone could pretend so they could stay out on leave. In the midst of it all, when I looked at things this way, I was *miserable*!

Put the right person in that environment, and they will *thrive*. They see people who need to provide for their families. They see employers who want to give to their employees. And they see opportunities to mend that work relationship. But I wasn't the right person. Not at that time, anyway. I was just claims adjusting. I was just doing a job. So were many of my coworkers. We depended on each other to get the job done, but many of us struggled to perform. Every time we went out for lunch, every single one of us complained about how much we hated claims adjusting. But we kept coming back. Maybe it was the money. I don't know.

There was this guy named Eric. He'd been here longer than some of us, and he absolutely hated the place.

"This place is the dump!" he cursed as he spat food from his mouth one day at lunch. "I've been here all this time. I'll probably be here forever." He took a big bite out of his chicken sandwich.

"Well, why?" I asked. His commentary was similar to yesterday's and last week's. "Why don't you just quit?" I blurted out.

The room fell silent. Everyone quit chewing their food and looked right at Eric. Slowly Eric put down his sandwich, wiped his hands in a napkin, and stared out the window.

"I hadn't thought of that."

Several weeks later, Eric turned in his resignation. I've never seen someone look so relieved as the day Eric walked out of the office for the last time. To my knowledge, he's been happy ever since. That wasn't my story, though. At least not yet. In my story, the husband and wife come home every night and cry themselves to sleep. And in the morning when we wake up, we lay on the bed with pillows over our faces to soak up even more tears.

"I don't want to go into work," my wife, Josie, said one morning, as she did *every* morning. "How long can I stay here in bed without being late?" She wanted to put off seeing the Basement as long as possible. Sometimes she left for work when it was dark and got home when it was dark. No sunlight for her. And I wasn't brightening her day with my set of challenges at the insurance place.

I Found My Calling in a Toilet Bowl

"I don't get it," I said, forcing myself to finally sit up. "We're both college graduates. *College!* Isn't there anything better out there for us than this . . . this . . . *kind of life, Jo?*"

"Maybe there is. Maybe there isn't. You ever think of that, Gerren? Maybe *this*"—Jo waved her hand in front of her tear-stained face—"is as good as it gets for us."

I looked away.

"I'm tired of seeing you like this. I'm tired of us waking up hating our lives. We're too young." I got up and stomped into the bathroom. "This *has* to stop."

"How, Gerren? And when?"

I looked in the mirror, out of her sight, and shrugged embarrassingly at myself as I whispered, "I don't know, Jo."

I had a number in my head—forty-five. We weren't even thirty years old yet. No kids, no plans, and no future. At least it didn't seem so, the way things were going.

When I was nine years old, I took a summer trip to Colorado with my grandmother and aunt. On the flight home to St. Thomas in the US Virgin Islands, I proclaimed out of the blue, "I want to retire at the age of forty-five."

They both laughed. I don't know why I said that. No one told me that people retire at sixty, sixty-five, or older. I just picked forty-five, and that's that. As a kid, I didn't know how I'd find financial freedom so young. And as a grown man crying every morning before work and every evening after, I still didn't. But that number remained front and center.

Growing up, I wasn't without hints at a prosperous future. My grandfather was a self-employed dentist. My father owned a marine store on St. Thomas where he sold boating parts and offered mechanical services to the fishing and marine industry in the islands. His brothers (my uncles) owned their own businesses, too. Maybe entrepreneurship coursed through my veins. My mother was a teacher, so you'd figure school was pretty easy. Nope. I fell off track, had bad grades, and got labeled the class clown.

One of my teachers in grade school took me aside after I'd disrupted the lesson (again).

"Gerren, you've got to do better. Do you understand? You've *got* to do better."

For a while after that, I got my grades back on track. *For a while*. By the time I reached tenth grade, I'd taken the seventh-grade science class four times. My younger sister sat in the front row. I sat in the back.

I lied to my friends about it. After lunch, I bragged, "Hey, I got a free period. See you later." But to my sister's class I went. Embarrassing.

The teacher who'd scolded me a few months prior didn't pressure me this time. Instead, he sent me to the school counselor to take a personality profile assessment. (Kids at that age should be playing ball and hanging out on the playground, not choosing a career, but that's a rant for another book.) The assessment looked at my strengths and weaknesses and recommended professions based on both. Apparently, my top strength was communication. And of course my number-one weakness was math. *Math.* I hated math then, and I still hate it today.

(*Hey! Did I ever tell you I hate math? Maybe it's numbers. They drain me.*)

I looked at the top-three recommended professions based on my assessment: coach, psychologist, or teacher. No, no way, and absolutely not. I definitely didn't want to be a conventional teacher and have to deal with knuckleheads like me in class. I saw how much work my mother put in to be an awesome teacher, and I just wasn't that committed. Yet.

"This can't be right," I told the school counselor on the way out. "I don't know how else I can use my skills, but these jobs aren't it. Not in their traditional forms, anyway."

Coach, psychologist, teacher, or whatever, I had no shot at a career if I didn't get my grades up. Then one of my other teachers (and soon-to-be mentor), Gordon Williams, sat down with me after school. He looked me calmly in the eye and said, "Gerren, you have to graduate with your class. Let's work toward it." Mr. Williams took my buddy Jonathan and me by the collar and made us study long enough to pass every grade-level test.

I don't know how we did it, but I owe my diploma to that man. When I graduated on time, one of my best friends, Sammy, wanted to join the military, so I packed a bag and circled the local recruiting center in red highlight on a paper map (back when they had those).

"That's noble, son, but absolutely not!" my parents said when I announced my plans. "You're going to college. We saved money for you to go, and you're going."

I applied at Columbia Union College (now Washington Adventist University) in Takoma Park, Maryland, near other relatives. I hadn't seen my cousins in years.

When the acceptance letter came, my parents asked me, "So what are you going to study? Psychology? Education?"

"Nope. Computer Science," I said proudly. The thing is, I had no interest in computers. But that was the hottest thing going on, so . . . Everybody else wanted to get into computers in the 1990s. In 1995, what better major to choose than the one on the rise? *Any* degree, actually. Nobody told me how many math classes computer science required. I failed my freshman year with a 2.1 GPA and brought the news home.

"Wait. Wait. Wait. What am I looking at here?" my mom asked. "I'm not having this. If this is how you're

I Found My Calling in a Toilet Bowl

going to spend our hard-earned money, bringing these grades home, you might as well consider paying for college yourself."

"Mom. I'm passing, am I not?" I said, not understanding what a GPA really was.

"If we're going to keep paying for you, you *must* do better, son."

I took a hard look at myself. Why was I failing? I wasn't focused. I was skipping classes to play table tennis, basketball, and pool. I acted as though I was free, but I was sent to college for a reason. There was something I was to prepare for, and I had to take this journey seriously. So I recalculated. I changed my mind-set, my focus, and began my new journey. I transferred my freshman-year credits to Strayer University in Washington, DC. At Strayer, I couldn't party all day in the dorms like I had at Columbia Union. At the time, the university offered only evening and weekend classes to fit working adults' busy schedules. In that environment, I found that I focused better.

I got a full-time job at Premier Kites in Hyattsville, Maryland, to help pay for college myself. During my few years there, I rose from stock clerk to warehouse manager. My friend Omar and I—along with other employees—increased packing and shipping output every single year. Meanwhile, I raised my grades to the high Bs and put a smile on my parents' faces. In 2001, I graduated debt-free and moved to Orlando, where my then girlfriend (now wife) accepted a job offer at a major hospital. I updated my résumé with my fancy new degree, sent copies all over Central Florida, and landed a job. A *minimum wage* job.

The day I got my first raise of fifteen cents, I told my supervisor, "I can't do this. I didn't work hard in college just to earn a few cents more than minimum wage. I quit." Not quite the best way to go about things, but this was my journey. One in which I'd have highs and lows.

I mailed out a second batch of résumés and found a *real* job—workers' compensation adjuster at an established insurance company with a full benefits package and a $35,000 annual salary. (That's $50,000 today, adjusting for inflation. I said I *hate* math. I didn't say I couldn't *do* math.)

I called my parents back home. "You won't believe it! Corporate America, here I come. I'm making $35,000 a year out of college. I've finally made it!"

"Congratulations!" Mom said. "Working in computers?"

"Uh, well, not exactly. I'll be doing workers' comp claims adjusting . . . on computers. So that counts, right?" I'm always being silly.

"So you're not using your degree, son?"

"No, I guess not. I'm just not finding jobs in my field, Mom. They're now saying they want people who have certifications."

"You have a degree, son."

I Found My Calling in a Toilet Bowl

"Mom! Thirty-five thousand dollars, remember?" I asked, upbeat.

The money wasn't enough. Let me rephrase that. Sure, it was enough for my bills, just not for my happiness. I worked that job for three miserable years.

One of my friends came over to my house and brought this drink called Ponche Kuba. He left the bottle behind that night, and I finished the rest the next morning on my way to work. Cold and creamy, it hit the spot. *I like this stuff. I really like this.* I opened the foil to my vegetarian griller sandwich.

I bought two more bottles on the way home from work that afternoon. From that day forward, I fit Ponche Kuba into my morning routine: get up, shower, get dressed, drink Ponche Kuba, eat a vegetarian sandwich, head out the door. By the time I reached work, that sense of dread left. I felt calm walking into the office, calm at my desk, and calm through lunch.

A few months later, Josie got up early with me one morning and saw me pouring that creamy goodness onto ice in a red SOLO cup.

"Um, babes? Where are you going with that?"

"To work," I said. "Like I always do every morning."

"*Every* morning?" Josie's jaw dropped. "You drink that *every* morning?"

"Yeah, I usually drink it on the way into work. Why? Do you want some?" I reached for a second cup.

"*No!*" Josie stepped to me. "Dude, you know this is alcohol, right? It's got rum in it."

"Seriously?" I grabbed the bottle and read the label. I never thought to before. "Says, 'Ponche Kuba Cream.'"

"Keep reading."

"'Ponche Kuba Cream'—Oh. 'Cream *Liqueur*."

"No wonder you've been so happy lately." Josie shook her head. "You're lucky you weren't stopped by the cops!"

That's when I realized I had a problem. A *big* problem. I threw the Ponche Kuba into the trash. The bottle, that is. After I finished it.

So that's how rough things are around here, I thought on the drive to work. *I never even (intentionally) drink alcohol, and here I am depending on it. No more rum for me.*

A few weeks into my Ponche Kuba detox, I took my wife out to dinner. The host walked us back to an open table for two where an employee was wiping down the table. He straightened the condiments and set down our silverware. The entire time, he didn't make eye contact. He didn't say anything. We just stood there. He turned to move on to the next table.

"Excuse me, sir," I said. "Thank you."

He looked at me, confused. "Huh? Why would you say that?"

"Well, you just cleaned our table. Actually, you didn't just clean the table. You prepared a nice place for my wife and I to have dinner, so thank you."

He broke a smile. His chest kicked up. "Yeah? I really did that?"

"Yeah. If you hadn't made it so nice, my wife and I wouldn't sit here. So thank you, sir."

He carried that grin to the next table. I saw a new sense of pride in his face. He wasn't just wiping down tables anymore—he was preparing a place for people to enjoy dinner. I got chills. I looked at Josie.

"I want to do that again."

Later that week, I worked out with my friend Keith at our local Planet Fitness, which happened to be a customer of Keith's part-time cleaning business. Every so often when his workload was heaviest, I'd help him out part-time so he could get home sooner and spend more time with his family.

While riding home one evening in the back seat of his Toyota Tundra, I found myself daydreaming. I stared up at the full moon.

"Why you so quiet?" Keith said with his island accent.

"I think I can do this," I said out loud.

"Do what?"

"I think I can do this cleaning thing. Full time, I mean. I think—I think I can start a janitorial company, too."

Keith laughed. "No, no, no! This is just side money, dude. Keep your day job."

"It's not about the money. I wouldn't compete with you. I don't even know if I'm cut out to be in business for myself. It's just . . ." I looked back up at the moon. *That guy at the restaurant. Wiping down tables. He totally changed when I thanked him. He became a whole new person*, I thought. *How many other opportunities are there to make people feel good about themselves? Especially people who work in less than appealing industries. Who else can I impact in that same way?*"

"Well, thanks for not trying to put me out of business, but that's not what I meant. Gerren, you dress up in suits all day at that insurance place. Why would you want to get down on your hands and knees, clean bathrooms, and stare at toilet bowls all day if you didn't have to? This is a part-time job, dude. I repeat, keep your day job."

"I hear you," I said. I sat quietly the remainder of the ride home.

Remember Eric. A few days after I told him he should quit, he turned in his resignation at work. That bastard! I wasn't angry at him. I was angry at myself. I thought he'd found freedom. The freedom I wanted.

"I'm so happy for you," I'd told him in confidence on his way out. "I hope it turns out to be the right decision. Good luck out there."

I hated my job even more.

"I need to make a change Jo," I said over dinner at home that night. Freezer meals. Neither of us had the energy to cook. "I need to make a difference. How can I do that sitting in a cubicle eight, sometimes ten hours a day? I'm just talking to people on the phone. As silly as this sounds, I want to be like that kid at the restaurant, meeting people and making life better for others."

"But what's the alternative to a secure job?" Jo picked at the vegetables in our so-called pasta medley. "Going into business for yourself is risky. Look at Keith. Sure, he's got all the Planet Fitnesses around here as customers, but it's his side hustle. You're talking about going all in. Are there any other positions available at your job now? I still want to have kids, and that requires stability and—"

"Of course it does, baby. I want kids, too. All the available leadership positions require more workers' comp experience, though. I'm just not that into sitting in a cubicle, talking to people who barely want to speak to me. I just need you to back me on this. I'm willing to do whatever I legally can to provide for us if this doesn't work. I'll go to work at McDonald's. I'll go to work anywhere. I *promise*, you will not go hungry. Let's do something risky while we still can, before we have kids. Let's try it. I just have to go after this now, or I never will."

"I know you'll do whatever it takes, and I won't go hungry. I've got your back. Always. But you keep saying 'this.' What's 'this'?"

"My own business," I said. "Any business. Maybe janitor work like Keith."

"Really? Cleaning toilets all day?"

"It's not just cleaning toilets. Remember the kid at the restaurant? He did more for us than just wipe down a table. He created a clean, fresh, and inviting environment. It doesn't matter, really. You know my ego is on the side when it comes to this. I want us to be happy. Whatever the future is, I don't want it to be us waking up crying in bed. We've got to shift gears. Recalculate where we're going."

"Okay. Okay, Gerren." Josie reached across the table and rubbed my shoulder. "I'll back you up on this. Let's look at our savings, insurance, put a plan together, and see what changing directions looks like. But can you do one thing first?"

"Anything."

"Have a talk with someone at the office. Maybe there's something else you can do there. A new opportunity that maybe you or he hadn't thought about. Maybe . . . maybe the future is closer than you think."

I Found My Calling in a Toilet Bowl

I agreed. At 8:01 the next morning, I knocked on my coworker Larry's office cubicle wall.

"What's up, Gerren?"

"Morning, Larry. Got a minute?"

"Yeah."

I sat in the chair closest to the cubicle entrance and leaned forward. "Larry, you know me. You were my supervisor for what, a year? So when you look at me, what do you see in me and my future here? Tell me. What do you think I do well? What am I good at? Because I want to do better. You see me here every day coming to work, trying to do my job."

Larry leaned back in his chair and glanced down at his open laptop. "Gerren, it's 8:02. We hired you to do a job. I need you to go back to your desk and do that job."

"But what do you see in me beyond *this* job? I figure, as a manager, you can see talent where it exists."

"Talent? *Talent?*" Larry snorted. "Clean up your to-do list and get on top of your claim filings, then we'll talk talent."

As a friend, I know he didn't mean harm. But that walk out of Larry's cubicle back to my desk was the longest hike of my life. My eyes were glazed over. All I saw were coworkers' heads bobbing slightly above the sea of cubicles. *I'm sinking.*

A few more weeks passed. I didn't strike up a conversation with a single coworker. Not since Larry. I was just walking the halls, moving paper, and delaying calls.

My new supervisor, Tiffany, called me over to her cubicle. "Gerren, you're falling behind. You need to either get the job done or get off the pot."

I walked back to my desk breathing heavy. I called Josie. "Jo," I said, deflated.

"Gerren? What's going on?"

"Jo," I said again.

She got the message. She took a deep breath. "Do it. I love you, Gerren."

I hung the phone up without saying another word, typed and printed a resignation letter, and walked back to Tiffany. I didn't knock on her cubicle wall this time.

"Tiffany"—I held up my letter—"I think I'm going to get off the pot." I slid the letter onto her desk.

Tiffany skimmed the first paragraph and shot to her feet. "No, no, I was just . . . not that I was kidding, but"—she chuckled—"I just wanted you to do better. You're a real asset to the company. To our team."

I shook my head. "No. You're right. This is me getting off the pot." And I left.

> ## 🖌 Pump Your Brakes
>
> Change, for many, is scary. But what do you do when everything around appears scarier? Have you ever been poked, poked some more, bumped, and pushed a bit? Sometimes we get annoyed with the thing . . . when in fact that thing was put there to get you moving. God has a different way of doing things. Go ahead, scream. Arrgghhhh . . . now jump!

Do What You Say You're Going to Do

Back, meet wall. *Either you do what you said you were going to do,* I thought on my last walk out. *Or suck up your pride and go back to Tiffany.* So I took the next step—I drove right to the local janitorial store and bought a backpack vacuum cleaner for $300. I spent another $200 on a mop, a bucket, Fabuloso, white terry-cloth towels, and a business license. I had my neighbor and friend Bob, who is an accountant, help me. That's it. A $500 start-up.

If I save everything I make, I can afford Pine-Sol and better cloths, I thought. *Then I'll take income from the business. Jo will understand.*

She did. She was the *only one* who did.

A month into me getting doors slammed in my face at every business in town, my mother-in-law joined us for dinner.

"Did you pick up any new clients today, son?"

"No. No, I didn't."

She put down her fork. "Maybe it's best for you to just go back to work for somebody. How can you come home and tell your wife you don't have any business?"

"Don't ever, *ever* ask me that question again!"

She jumped back in her seat.

"I'm sorry, but I can't have anybody around me doubting what I'm doing. I'm committed, I'm driven, and I'm willing to do whatever it takes to start this journey off well."

Rude? Sure. But when you're driven and you're doing all that you know how to, it's tough hearing people doubt your decisions. Being in business is difficult by itself. There's no need to surround yourself with people who will judge you. *I'm trying here, woman!* I thought to myself. I recognize I didn't have a whole lot going for me yet. But man! Imagine a bald, six-foot-four black guy with a goatee showing up at your office or home.

"Hello, would you like me to clean your office?"

"You don't look like a janitor," several receptionists said with a straight face.

"What's a janitor supposed to look like?"

They'd think for a minute and glance at the door I'd just walked through. "Well, not you. I'm going to have to ask you to leave, sir."

Maybe It's Me, Not You!

What's going on? Friends always joked that I was "the Angry Black Man" because I tend to frown when I get lost in thought. Maybe my face turned people off. Or maybe I wasn't the problem. Maybe a different approach would get me my first account. What approach that was, I didn't know . . . yet.

The next prospect on my list kicked me out of his lobby before I finished my elevator pitch.

"Not interested. No loitering," he said.

On my way out, the UPS guy showed up. My prospect turned around and waved.

"Hey, Steve!" He grinned from ear to ear. "You're here! Thanks for the packages. How are you doing? How's the family?"

Really? You practically slam the door in my face, but you open up your business to this guy with a million smiles? Maybe . . . maybe I need to be a UPS guy. Then businesses will give me the time of day.

> **Pump Your Brakes**
> What is it that you really want? Is it the sale? Is it the job? Is it happiness? A chance? A conversation? If I hadn't focused on the fact that all I really wanted was acceptance (so I could prove I'm worth having around), I would've lost the gift of the UPS guy. What's happening around you? Step back from needing the ultimate goal. What do you need next to get you closer? What can you learn from others who may be "doing it better"?

At that exact second, a Courier Express car drove by. And like that guy at the restaurant, a smile crept across my face, and I lit up!

I called Josie immediately. "Babes! You know that company, Courier Express? They're like UPS except they hire independent contractors to run deliveries."

"What about them?"

"I'm going to be a courier."

"You're *what*? What are you talking about?"

"Listen to this. I go to all these businesses, and I can't get past the front desk. They throw me out or ask me to leave. Either way, I keep coming home empty-handed. But these delivery guys show up, and the people are all smiles. If I were to become a courier, I could get in the door by delivering a package."

She backed me up. I called Courier Express immediately.

"Hey, are you guys hiring?"

"Yeah, we're hiring."

"I'd like a full-time job."

"You understand the average contractor earns the equivalent of a part-time income."

"It's okay, I don't mind."

"Well, when can you start?"

"Right now."

It was that easy. Courier Express hired me. All I wanted to do was replicate the interaction I saw Steve have with my prospect. I just wanted to get in the door so people could see how nice a guy I was. I made business cards for my janitorial services—Clean Slate Janitorial Services—and kept them in a little plastic case I got from Walmart.

> **Pump Your Brakes**
>
> The wind can be your friend—and your foe. Imagine you're in a sailboat, and you need the wind to take you to shore. If the wind is blowing against you, you can get frustrated—or you can turn the sail and use it to your advantage. Pause and take a look at what's been pushing you. How can you use it to get where you're trying to go?

The first delivery route Courier Express assigned to me included major organizations like the regional hospital. I knew I couldn't offer to clean facilities that big by myself, so I requested a different route with more small businesses. My daily schedule sent me to some of the same businesses who accused me of loitering just days earlier. When I walked in *this* time with a package under my arm and a clipboard in my hand, receptionists smiled.

"Oh, I'm so glad you're here!"

After I handed over the package with a smile, I pointed to the lobby floor, windows, and light fixtures. "Does anybody clean your building?"

"Actually, no. Do you know someone?"

"As a matter of fact, I do." I put my hand into front pocket. "Here's my card."

"Wow, you clean, too?"

I Found My Calling in a Toilet Bowl

"Here's the deal," I said. "I'm not trying to take work away from anyone else. If I can help you improve . . . get more of what you're looking for, would that help?" I kept it literally that simple.

"Yes it would, young man. Can you give us a call to schedule that? Let me get you my card before you go."

I went from zero clients to five just like that. I quit Courier Express, bought the Pine-Sol, and found my rhythm. Over the next six years, I grew the business to over twenty clients—all by myself. I was better off going solo than drowning in that office. But better isn't best. Sleeping in my car got old. Working twelve to fifteen hours a day, six days a week got old. Doing something that didn't make me come alive got old. I made great money—quadruple my claims-adjuster salary. I wasn't miserable, but I wasn't happy, either. I thought quitting your job and being your own boss was supposed to be a "Boss Move."

Then I remembered that high school assessment.

Communicator. Coach. Psychologist. Teacher.

What was I missing?

> **Pump Your Brakes**
>
> "Practice? You're just talking about practice." I remember Allen Iverson's press conference where he suggested practice was a waste of time. He blew the world away. But no matter where you are in your career, you have an opportunity to work on some skill. Maybe it's listening, questioning, praising, encouraging, or focusing. There are plenty more. What skill can you work on right now? You may think it's not what gets you out of your current situation, but could it be that you'll need that soft skill at your next stop? Quiet your mind for a moment. What if you need that skill . . . at your next stop?

One night while plunging a toilet that refused to flush employees' business, I asked myself two questions: *What am I really doing? What if a job isn't just a job? What if a job is a vehicle to do what I'm good at, or what I was created to do, ultimately making the world a better place? What if? What if? What if?*

I cleaned up the stall, made that floor spotless with my upgraded cleaning solutions, and wheeled my janitorial trolley into the owner's office to vacuum. I didn't vacuum—yet. "What if? What if?" I kept repeating, reminding myself of this new way of thinking. I walked up to his desk and read the titles of his books, magazines, and newsletters—all titles about business, leadership, and management. I wrote them all down on the back of an unused invoice. Then I vacuumed.

First thing the next morning, I drove to Borders bookstore and got my hands on as many of those books as I could find. I read, took notes, and memorized a few key takeaways from each in between building cleanings. I wasn't sure when I could use what I learned, but about a week after my trip to Borders, the opportunity presented itself. When I passed the owner's office on my way to that same restroom, I saw a light on.

"Hey, John!" I popped my head in. "Why are we working so late tonight?"

"Oh, the economy. Things are just rough, Gerren. We have employees to pay and clients we're struggling with. I guess the stress adds up if you don't get ahead, you know?"

Now's my chance. "What do you stress about in particular? If you don't mind talking while I clean."

"Sure. I could use a break from all this." John rolled up his sleeves. "Well, as you know, we do accounting for small- and medium-size businesses. But what we really specialize in is tax planning."

"Where do you want your business to go?" I got out my duster and cleaned his bookshelves.

John let out a deep belly laugh. "*Ha!* Anywhere but where we're headed now."

"You said you're stressed." I cleaned his framed diplomas and certifications a little slower than usual. "Looking at this from a high level, why do you think things aren't going in the right direction? From the outside, you guys seem to have a really successful business, and I see all the effort you make."

"Well, it seems like every quarter there's a new regulation. These regulations . . . well, they're like hurricanes. They come through the business and send all our hard work flying in different directions. In fact, I'm here tonight to pick up the pieces for one of our top clients. They're in hot water with the IRS over last year's taxes."

"At the end of the day, what got you here won't get you there." I quoted the title of the leadership book by Marshall Goldsmith. "Maybe you can overcome this problem if you look at all the new laws not as threats, but as opportunities." I paraphrased my notes from the book. "You see what I mean?"

"An *opportunity*, not a *threat* . . ." John nodded along. "Wait a second. How would you know that?" He rummaged through the papers on his desk and pulled out his hardback copy of *What Got You Here Won't Get You There*. "Have you—have you ever read this book?"

"Yes, sir."

"Huh." John's bushy eyebrows twitched. He stared down at the book, his head tilted to the side. "I wouldn't think a janitor reads business books. Then again, you did show up to our first meeting in a suit."

"I'm just your janitor, John." I shrugged and walked back to my trolley in the doorway. I did this several times with John—sharing little nuggets of information I'd learn. I'd ask him questions that would get his mind rolling and his mouth going, and I'd soak that stuff up like I was breathing air. And every time, I would leave the room and have my voice trail off down the hall.

"I'm just your janitor, John."

Until that one day . . .

"You know what?" John got up. "Come sit down. Right here." He pointed to the client's chair facing his desk.

I put my duster back on the trolley and rubbed sanitizer on my hands.

"Okay, Gerren. This is the problem we're having. It's more than just the IRS issue. Our business model can't really handle our big clients' needs. If we keep letting them down, there's a good chance they'll *all* take their business to a competitor here in town. What would you do?"

I glanced back at my trolley. "I'll give you an example. You see that Pine-Sol there?"

"Yeah."

"When I started this business, I wanted to give my clients the best experience, the best cleaning products, and the best image possible so they could impress everyone who walked through their doors. The whole nine."

John nodded.

"But I was in hustle mode, or what Eric Ries calls 'lean start-up.' I couldn't afford the Pine-Sol yet, so I stocked up with Fabuloso. It's cheaper per bottle, but I have to use more of it on every job. So in the short-term, I was making a bigger profit. But now that I've got a full book of business, I can afford to make strategic purchases."

"Like Pine-Sol."

"Exactly."

"Wow." John sat back and stared up at the ceiling. "In that case, maybe subcontracting makes sense. It's less profitable now, but we'll be able to meet more needs."

"And that allows you to grow, land even bigger accounts, and move forward from there."

"Yes. *Yes!* You just articulated in one minute what I've been struggling with for *weeks*." John shot to his feet. "I know what I have to do now. Thank you so much,"—he shook my hand—"*Coach Gerren*." Now I didn't fully comprehend what I'd just shared. And frankly, the information may not have been what experts would recommend. Heck! I didn't even know how to really run my own business, but I was practicing a number of things. (Think about that for a bit, and we'll get into it later on in the book.)

I Did It Again!

I left John's office and wheeled my trolley into the restroom with the biggest, stupidest grin. I looked at myself in the mirror. *Gerren, I think you just found your calling, dude.* I grabbed my plunger off the trolley and got to work on the usual problem in stall number two. *You're in the right place, Gerren. And at the right time. Shoot! You're in the right place, Gerren! Cleaning this toilet allows me to have those types of conversations! Let's goooo!*

Staring into that toilet bowl at John's company, I realized that a job isn't just a job—it's a vehicle. And I already had both hands on the wheel. So I put my foot on the pedal and never looked back. More than a decade after that conversation, I've worked my way up from Clean Slate's sole janitor to staff supervisor to operations manager to CEO. Along the journey, I've taught employees each aspect of the job, mentored them to bigger and better careers, and coached fellow entrepreneurs to adopt high-performance psychology and get out of their own way . . . and befriended the Panera Police in the process.

Coach, psychologist, teacher. That's me!

If you look at jobs as vehicles/opportunities to do pretty cool things, the things you were gifted to do, to reach your one true calling, the world is wide open. Stop! Don't read over what I just shared. Slap yourself if you need to. Look around. You can do *anything* you want. Just make the commitment to grow along the way. Long-term, I may not remain in the cleaning industry. Who knows? I might ride this wave until I see an opportunity to sell the business to an employee I've taught, coached, and mentored.

"You take it," I might one day say. "I've created systems and processes in the business—now go ahead and improve on them. Make this business *your* vehicle."

If that moves me closer to happiness—the ultimate goal—then I've completed my assignment, and it's time to move on to the next one. I could probably make rugs or sell phones for a living and still find opportunities to live out my calling of teaching, coaching, and mentoring. If I'd looked beyond the job titles on that assessment, I would've found my calling much, *much* earlier. Still, I find myself doing what I'm called to do, set to retire at forty-five, and begin teaching hundreds of students, professionals, and business owners every year how to find their callings, too.

The truth is, I took the slow road to my calling—but you don't have to. If I can find my calling cleaning toilets, you can find yours right where you are today. I drove what some may call one of the most unattractive jobs—janitor work—toward my real passions. Now I get to be a coach, psychologist, and teacher every single day. But I get paid like a CEO.

I've made a lot of turns on this journey, including a lot of wrong ones. But a few specific turns *always* paid off and took me closer to happiness. I wrote this book to help you avoid my mistakes, steer clear of the detours, and get on the fast track to your calling—and *stay* there. I call these specific turns the **Five-Turn Fast Track Framework**™.

So if you're ready to find your calling faster than you ever thought possible—and feel fulfilled, happy, and inspired every day when you get out of bed—get behind the wheel. Buckle up. Adjust your mirror.

Next stop, your calling.

Key Point

Doing something different can be tough. What's also tough is looking at your current environment and the role you're playing in it. Consider what it would be like to stop blaming others and your surroundings for what's happening, because quite frankly, they're doing what they're supposed to. Use those opportunities to pivot and grow.

Action Steps

1. Take the Fast Track Your Calling™ Assessment.
2. Jot down how you're using or can use your strengths in your current job.
3. Have a conversation with your supervisor (or clients) about how you believe you can use your strengths to help them solve their challenges in new ways. See what opportunities open up for you. Then snuggle into your zone!

Chapter 2

Why You (Still) Haven't Found Your Calling

You're driving down the road. The GPS on your phone guides your every turn. You get lost in thought. You turn on the radio, switch to your go-to station, and hum along to a familiar song.

"*Your destination will be on the right.*"

Great! You're almost there. You turn down the volume and keep your eyes peeled for addresses and signs.

"*You have arrived.*"

Wait . . . I have? Your heart picks up. You check your mirrors. Traffic behind you keeps you from slowing down or stopping in the road to take your time and look. *Where in the world is this place?* You look to your left. Maybe the GPS was wrong? *Nothing over there.*

You pull to the right shoulder, turn on your hazard lights, and slow down. You had in mind what your destination looked like—what it's supposed to look like, at least. *But this isn't it!*

You grab your phone. The GPS destination marker confirms your arrival. *I must have the wrong address.* So there you sit on the side of the road waiting, car still running. *You look back at the address, confirm that it was written down correctly, and hit "Go."*

"You have arrived."

Now what?

Why Is It So &#$% Hard to Find Your Calling?

Most people never find their callings. Most people set off on a journey to find what they're meant to do, then just sit idling at what they *thought* was their calling. Forty or fifty years later, they retire from the pursuit altogether.

Whenever I talk to audiences of entrepreneurs or students, I hear the three same reasons over and over—three reasons why it's so hard to find your calling. The **first reason** people never find a career or a profession they find fulfilling is they follow other people's advice. Too many of us are driving to other people's addresses, pursuing other people's callings. I chose computer science as my college major because it was the hot new field, not because computer programming put a smile on my face. I guess the college admissions counselors persuaded me against my better judgment. Beware the advice of people who tell you what to do based on why *they* would do it.

My business attorney, Audrey K. Chisholm, Esq., refused to follow other people's career maps.

"I want to study law and be an attorney," she told her friends years before attending university.

"Ew, *law*? Why do you want to be a lawyer? Law is so boring!" they said.

If she'd taken their feedback to heart, she would've deviated from her destination. Because she didn't, she gets to represent Fortune 500 companies. Today, she boasts a 100 percent success rate for federal trademark registrations and a 100 percent success rate for 501(c)(3) nonprofit approvals by the IRS. How many attorneys do you know are boasting 100 percent success rates? Why do you think *she* can? Maybe, just maybe, she has certain skills that allow her to perform that assignment at such a high level. Think about it. Years from now, after you've found your calling and made history, will it matter what your friends said to you yesterday?

"Gerren, this is a bad idea. You dress so well! You could work anywhere. You shouldn't be cleaning toilets," friends and family told me when I started Clean Slate.

They were looking only at outside appearances, thinking only a business with a perceived status would bring me happiness. I have friends who earn literally six, even seven figures working at these so-called higher status companies, but some are just as miserable as I was at the claims-adjusting job. They feel like they can't quit because they've already built a lifestyle they have to support. And if they leave their miserable job to do something different, they're afraid they'll lose their spouse, their insurance, their homes, and go broke. Make no mistake about it. That's a strong possibility. What's the alternative?

Dare to Be a Daniel.

If I had listened to family and friends who laughed at my janitorial services start-up idea, I probably wouldn't be a CEO who gets to teach, coach, and mentor every day—my one true calling. Sure, it's not perfect. What job is? There are some days I get frustrated with my employees, with my business, or even just the work itself. But even with the challenges of running a business, I'm happy *every single day* because I get to do what I love. Your calling isn't utopia. But at the end of the day, there's *nowhere else* I'd rather be because I enjoy doing what comes naturally—teaching, coaching, and mentoring. It doesn't even feel like work. I remember speaking to my brother Guilderoy one day.

"Dude, I hate feeling the way that I'm feeling. I mean, who am I?" he asked. "Bro, you solve problems. You're the guy! Damn the title. You solve people's problems with integrity. Do that consistently and watch the amount of people who call you."

My brother was caught in the trap that many people often find themselves in. He thought for a moment he had to have a title in order to be recognized as someone worth speaking to. Every book I read, I shot him a text. "Check this book out. Here's how it helped me. Maybe you'll find a nugget in there." Some he'd read, and others he didn't get to . . . yet. He read at his pace, based on the problems he needed to solve. Now he's one of the government's go-to guys for some of their needs. Hey! He still doesn't have a fancy title. He just goes by Guilderoy Sprauve. That's a powerful title in my eyes!

If instead you feel like you'd rather be *anywhere else*, something is wrong!

Last Thanksgiving my wife sent me to pick up a pumpkin pie at Costco. "We need pumpkin pie, babe," she said. "Nothing else." Clear instructions to navigate the strategic traps of that big box store.

As I strolled the aisles among the hustling lunchtime crowd, I saw a former claims-adjusting coworker, Jeanine, inspecting fruits. She also happened to be my very first Clean Slate client.

"Heeeey!" she called out.

"Jeanine!" We shared a huge hug.

"Gerren, I haven't seen you in person in a while. I mean, I follow you online, but . . ." The joy fell from her face. "You know, you're always talking about callings and passion. Gerren, I hate my job! I *hate* it, Gerren. I. Hate. It." She bared her teeth. "I *love* what I do, but I *hate* my job."

If I got a buck for every conversation that began like that, oh my! How rich I would be.

"What's going on? Why do you say *hate*?" I asked.

"A lot is happening in the industry," Jeanine said. "Things are changing. The company gets me frustrated. I just—I just feel like I'm getting too old deal with all of these changes. And the market is looking for young folks. It's high turnover."

"Where does that leave you?"

"Actually, I plan to retire in the next four years. I won't really 'retire,'" she said, making air quotes. "I'll always work because I believe I can help people. I love what I do!"

"That's great to hear, J," I said. "I love that. We've got gifts to share. No point in hiding our talents under a bushel. I always remember you being so good at what you do. I even remember hearing you in the sea of cubicles back in the day. Always very animated and passionate. Fact is, your kind of joy *every* employer wants in their staff."

"Thank you, Gerren. Means a lot coming from you. So many years have gone by, I guess something has chiseled away that passion. Right after you left,

I thought about going independent and doing my own thing, too. My own claims-adjusting business."

"Really?" I was stunned. "That was . . . more than a decade ago. What happened? Why didn't you do it?"

"Well, I sat on the dream for a while. Then I got in touch with this lawyer and showed him my business plan and—"

"Hold up! You wrote a *business plan*?"

"Oh, yeah, Gerren. Like I said, I was serious about it. I hated things about my job back when you left, and I hate it today," Jeanine said. "Anyway, my lawyer advised me against starting a business. He told me it'd take three to five years to get things going. I thought, 'Well, that's a long time to go without steady income,' so I gave up on the idea."

"All because your lawyer said you should?"

"Yes, but I do think he's right. It's just not . . . it's not . . ." Jeanine quickly checked her watch. "It's just not practical. Anyway, I've got to get back to work, Gerren. It was great seeing you."

I've got to get back to work, Gerren. Those words haunted me as I finished up my shopping. Jeanine shared her frustration and her dream, and there she went, back to the place that was killing her passion over and over every day. All because she followed other people's advice. I wish more people followed the wisdom in their own hearts instead.

The **second reason** people get stuck and never find their callings is they confuse *callings* with *titles*. Like "Coach," "Psychologist," "Teacher." Those job titles from my assessment threw me off the road to my calling. Maybe *you've* taken a strengths assessment, looked at the results, and said, "*Huh?*"

I confused "Coach" with "coaching." On the flip side, if I'd refused to go by "Janitor," I never would have been able to enjoy doing what I do best. Who knew scrubbing floors and cleaning toilets would put me where I get to coach, teach, and mentor? Back in my claims-adjusting days, my goal to retire at forty-five seemed impossible with a job like teacher or psychologist. But those titles weren't my calling. They were hints that told me what I was good at and what I would truly enjoy doing. Once I got into the right vehicle and started driving, my calling wasn't as far away as I thought.

On the other hand, I heard the story of a woman who had earned not one, not two, but *six* college degrees to pursue what she *thought* was her one true calling. The day she submitted her PhD thesis was the day she decided to go into a different field. She'd fallen in love with the job titles in her chosen field, but she hated the work itself. I feel her pain. Completing college was anticlimactic for me. I never picked up my computer science degree. I didn't even attend my graduation, so my parents never got to celebrate my accomplishment. My mother doesn't like to hear me say this, but I always say, "I went to school to learn how to learn, not to gain a degree."

Granted, no one wants to know a person spent money on just learning, but I've never worked a day in my life in computers and have no desire to. I have, however, completed all requirements for the degree. For what it's worth . . .

The **third reason** people fall short of our callings is we think our calling is supposed to find *us*. You know the saying "delayed gratification"? You put off an immediate reward—money, success, happiness—so that (supposedly) you'll benefit much more later on. I see an awful lot of people delay their callings.

"Good things come to those who wait," they say. "Patience is a virtue."

People who follow this advice stay stuck in a miserable career. They cry every morning and every night (just like I used to), but they don't do anything to improve their circumstances. What are they waiting for? The fact is, your calling isn't going to come to you. The universe doesn't work that way! When you climb in the car and punch an address into your GPS, the destination doesn't come to you. *You* drive *there*. It's up to you to go out and find your calling. It's only logical.

So quit putting off your destiny. Why defer happiness to years down the road? Let's get you happy *now*. Money will come, and the journey to your calling doesn't have to be miserable. But how do you find this new destination? How do you even begin to look for your calling?

> **Pump Your Brakes**
>
> When you get out of college, the first thing you do is what? Find a job! That's the thing—we're always focused on finding a job. That's it. As opposed to what you really want to do. I get it. You want to explore. So why not explore? Don't make your goal to just "find a job"! Because then everything you do is attached to the job you get—the phone, the car, the house, the spouse, the kids. You're stuck. So why not pause after college so you don't get on that gerbil wheel? Prepare for the journey ahead so you hit the ground running in the right direction. Network. Build relationships. Job shadow. Interview people in the profession you might want to try. You can't figure it out on your own. So have a dialogue with people doing what you think you might want to do.

The Five-Turn Fast Track Framework™—The First Turn—Map

Your first turn in the **Five-Turn Fast Track Framework**™ is to look at your **map**—the map of life. Where, exactly, is your calling? It's time to find your destination, determine the address, punch it into your GPS, and start driving.

To make sure you're always headed in the right direction in your career (and your life), you're going to use a different kind of GPS. Not the one you find on your phone or those old devices on the clearance rack at your local electronics store. Your GPS to find your calling on the map is your **Gutsy Purpose Statement**. With one sentence, you'll not only know your life purpose—the very reason you exist on this planet—but you'll be able to turn any job, any career, any profession into a vehicle to drive you closer to your calling.

So how do you write your Gutsy Purpose Statement? Go back to when you were a kid. Remember when you were seven years old and announced to the world your crazy dream?

"I want to be a _____ when I grow up!"

Then you cupped your hand over your mouth and looked around because even at seven years old you knew that was crazy.

You may be thinking, *I didn't know anything as a kid. I hadn't experienced much yet. How could what I said at seven mean much of anything to my future?* Stay with me. The fact is, what you said as a kid was unfiltered by naysayers, the people who have "But" to say.

"But you're too small."

"But you're not that smart."

"But no one in our family has graduated before."

"But there's no money in that." (I absolutely hate this one!)

Sometimes you want to scream, *"Shut up with all your buts!"* but that would be inappropriate, wouldn't it? Step away from those thoughts (and screams) for a moment. Imagine just lying down while looking up at the sky.

What did you want to be when you grew up? Whatever it was, that dream contains truth that the world tells you to suppress. I believe in that dream because it's yours. Maybe you don't want to say it out loud, so write it down somewhere before someone suggests you keep your day job or worse yet say, "Don't be silly!" Because chances are you'll hear naysayers.

"It's not practical."

"It's so hard to get that job."

"You're in for a lifetime of heartache."

Whether your dream was to be an actor or an astronaut, don't believe the naysayers. Hold on to that dream for now.

Okay, let's go back to that moment in your childhood or adult life when you saw some type of problem that you wanted to solve. It was probably a moment when inspiration struck. What were five things about that job or that moment that excited and/or intrigued you? What did you see? What did you feel? What did you experience? Who did you do it with? What did you accomplish together?

Maybe this is a story you're afraid to tell. Maybe you've buried those feelings so deep that even you can't find them. I want you to set aside anything and everything from your mind that might hold you back. Close your eyes and just remember—no restrictions. *Shhhh*. Maybe you need to put the book down for a moment, go into a quiet room or space. Go ahead. You really need this.

Got those five things? What do you like about each of those five things? Let your imagination run wild, like you're a kid again. Open your mind wide. Nobody's looking. And it really doesn't matter if anyone is.

I'll give you an example. My daughter Maddie wants to be a dentist when she grows up.

"What do you see yourself doing?"

"Making people taste bubble gum!" she told me, referring to her flavored fluoride treatments. Maddie is six years old.

"What do you like about that?"

"I get to take care of people."

"What kind of people? Kids? Adults?"

"Not kids. Adults. Old people. When I'm a dentist, I get to take care of old people because old people take care of us."

Bingo. Maybe Maddy will in fact go to dental school someday, but right behind her dream is the desire to care for aging adults. *That*, in all likelihood, is her true calling—the address of her destination on life's journey. (I'll be old one day, Maddy. I hope you'll take care of Daddy.) Whether she's cleaning seniors' teeth or serving them in any of a hundred different ways, she'll have a smile on her face because that's her truth.

Check this out! Maddy also loves to draw. She'll pull up a YouTube video and draw what she sees. I sit back and look at the detail and smile. I can't even draw the things she draws so well. What I see is her creative mind going to work. To be an exceptional dentist, she could need some creative juices. Are you getting this? I'm looking forward to how she puts it all together. But you better believe I'm going to nurture it.

Don't look at being a dentist as meaning you just have to go to dental school and study what they tell you. Practice your creativity muscles now. You may find a mouth that needs reconstruction, and you, like Maddy, will be well equipped to come up with a crazy idea to help. You can do this! But you have to step back and look at your map.

What's meaningful about *your* five things? In what ways are you contributing to the world beyond yourself? If you wanted to be a movie star when you grew up, maybe what you find meaningful is keeping the arts alive. If you wanted to be a cowboy, maybe you really wanted to work in the outdoors. Told everyone you were going to be a superhero? Maybe you're passionate about saving the innocent from harm. Knew you would be the world's first princess turned race car driver? Maybe what you really are is a leader at heart with an affinity for risk-taking.

> ### 🖊 Pump Your Brakes
> Ever been on a train? When you're on a train, you pass by many sights that pique your curiosity. You wish you could get off and see some of them. But you're on a train. So you can't. That's why I prefer the drive. I say, pull over and check out those interesting things! Exploring brings me happiness. It's the same in our careers. It's okay to pull over, explore, and try something new. The joy is in the journey, not the job title.

Whatever it is you find most meaningful about your crazy childhood dream or that moment that gave you goosebumps, flip that around into your Gutsy Purpose Statement. Saw yourself becoming an astronaut? That job title isn't your GPS. Your Gutsy Purpose Statement might be, "I help people appreciate our place in the universe." If you did that, how many different things can you do now? How many areas/industries can you help people appreciate our place in the universe? As my daughter grows up, her dentistry dream may very well give way to, "I help take care of those who take care of us."

If you're honest with yourself when you write out your Gutsy Purpose Statement, you'll see your calling. Your address. Your map. Not your parents' map. Not your teachers' map. Not your bosses' map. *Yours.* No more excuses. You can recalculate your route wherever you are and still reach your destination (I'll show you how in Chapter 3). But it's your job to punch in your new address and move in the right direction. I assure you, if you follow your new GPS instructions, you'll spring forward toward your goals so much faster than anyone else, and you'll turn any job—even janitorial work—into a vehicle that takes you to your calling.

So what's *your* toilet bowl?

Key Point

If you want to be the best at something, you have to practice. Figure out what you want to be good at and begin finding ways to practice right where you are. Remember, you don't need a title to practice.

Action Steps

1. What problems have you ever dreamed about solving?
2. What were five things about those activities that excited or intrigued you?

3. What is meaningful to you *now* about those five things?

4. Write each of those things as a Gutsy Purpose Statement beginning with, "I help . . ." Play around. Have fun with this!

    - e.g., "I help people create clean, fresh, inviting environments." (Clean Slate Janitorial Services) "I help women feel beautiful." (Hairdresser) "I help machines better serve people." (Mechanical Engineer) "I help people protect their family's and business's privacy." (Information Technology Security) "I help people harvest the fruit of their labor." (Accountant) "I help healthcare professionals stay safe so they can help their patients get better." (Physician Contract Manager)

Chapter 3
Closer Than You Think

"That's not a quick stop," I said to my wife. "That's what we call a *detour*."

She pulled up her GPS app. "Let's see about that."

We were on our fifth day of vacation in Austin, Texas, and had just dropped off our friends—Darryl, Marixa, and their kids—at the airport.

"So where exactly do Keisha and George live?" I asked.

"Somewhere in Texas. I bet it's far. This state is so huge! She'd be so excited to see us in her neck of the woods. We were like *this* back in college." Josie held up two fingers. "You remember, don't you?"

"Uh, yeah!" I said. "Of course I remember. You got her address?"

"Yeah, right here." Josie scrolled through recent texts on her phone. "I'll punch it in the GPS."

"Hold on—I didn't mean we should *go* there. Like, right now."

"I just want to see how close we are."

"Fine." I peeked at our kids in the rearview mirror. Both squealed in excitement over our vacation.

"Where are we going to next?" our daughter Morgan asked.

"I don't know yet, Morg. We leave for home tomorrow, so I'm hoping we can connect with Aunty Keisha and Uncle George at some point. We'll see."

"Hey, look!" Josie smiled. "It *is* a quick stop!" She held up the GPS in front of me: "58 min."

"Really? That's it?" I felt bad. "Well, in that case . . ."

"Let's hit the road. Fort Hood it is." Josie sent the coordinates to the dashboard GPS, and off we went.

I guess we're closer than I thought.

Find Your Nineveh

If you ever attended Sabbath School (or Sunday School) as a kid, chances are you heard the story of Jonah. A prophet of Israel, Jonah was called to preach in distant lands. His first assignment: Nineveh, a city in modern-day Iraq.

Hold on—that can't be right, Jonah must've thought. *The people of Nineveh* kill *prophets. I don't want to be a martyr!*

So Jonah ran away to a local port looking for a ship to take him in the opposite direction—literally. At that time in the ancient world, the town of Tarshish on the west coast of modern Spain was about as far away as you could get!

Jonah set sail for Tarshish, leaving the road to Nineveh behind. His little plan, however, didn't pan out. Remember the part about a huge storm that caused chaos among his fellow passengers—the people around him? Ultimately they got sick of his baggage and threw him overboard. Then a fish swallowed him alive and threw him back up on land. Quite a story.

God never called Jonah to martyrdom, just evangelism. But fearful Jonah ran away from his calling, so he didn't find that out until it was almost too late. His destiny was closer than he thought. So was mine.

"Coach."

"Psychologist."

"Teacher."

Hold on—those can't possibly be right, I'd thought as a young man. So I ran away, too. Maybe not to the ends of the earth, but I studied computers in college and spent years in claims adjusting. Like Jonah, I fled my calling because I *misunderstood* it. I had no idea how close I really was to finding my happy place—and earning an amazing living. I looked at those things in a common form, the way I saw everyone else using those talents and didn't realize, at first, that I could be as creative as I wanted to be. I saw my natural abilities as a dream job that was just that—a dream. Something way, way out there that would take a long time to reach. *Too* long. So I settled into mediocrity (for me). If I'd known to look for the common thread among those top career paths, I would've started out differently. *I wouldn't have run away to Tarshish clear across the Mediterranean!*

It's not that I didn't have good opportunities. While I worked at the warehouse in Hyattsville, Maryland, to pay tuition, I got promoted to manager and successfully led a team much older than me. After college, I found myself speaking on behalf of my coworkers and helping them deal with personal issues and professional challenges. Now that I have Clean Slate Janitorial Services, I've found my Nineveh. I have employees I can teach, share experiences with, and help find their Nineveh. They're my students in my classroom. I show people how to find their calling. I'm their career coach who's made mistakes so they don't have to. And I help employees deal with their issues. I may not be a psychologist, but I bring value like one. I realized I could live my calling—communicating, teaching, motivating, encouraging—in *any* environment. If only I'd known back then how close I really was.

> **Pump Your Brakes**
>
> What do you enjoy doing? I don't care if you like reading spreadsheets or playing Tetris. Why do you enjoy that? Got an answer? Okay, what if you were supposed to use that skill at your job, with your friends, or at church? If you were supposed to read spreadsheets or play Tetris regularly because you enjoyed it, what would that mean to you? It's okay to get paid for what comes naturally.

Not a day goes by I don't encounter a fellow Jonah—somebody taking a detour away from their calling because they have no clue how close they *already* are.

I once asked the guy at a Chick-fil-A drive-through, "Why do you like working here?"

"I don't!" He laughed.

"Dude, why? What is it you don't like? I feel like I could learn so much from Chick-fil-A as a business. Plus, it's always a pleasant experience. I enjoy the food. Every time I say thank you, you guys say, 'My pleasure." I want *my* employees showing that kind of spirit."

"Yeah, well, I don't want to learn anything," he said. "I want to go home."

"How long have you been working here?" I asked over the cars honking behind me. I still hadn't ordered.

"I've been here for a couple of months."

"How about this? Would you mind coming to my office and sharing your Chick-fil-A experience with me? I'll give you fifty bucks. I'll bet you've learned a lot more than you think. And I *guarantee* what you've learned is a lot more valuable than you think."

"Sure," he said.

The kid never showed. Too bad. I was willing to *pay* someone to teach me how to train my employees like Chick-fil-A. Just because you run a fast food drive-through doesn't mean you can't change the world. No matter what vehicle you're in, you can bring value to people's lives. You can put your strengths to use. Don't run away from Nineveh and sink your career.

A few weeks before I started writing this book, I struck up a conversation with a young girl sitting in an auditorium filled with other college students.

"What do you want to be when you grow up?" I asked her.

"I want to be a hairdresser."

"Interesting," I said. "Why do you want to be a hairdresser?"

"I just want to make women feel beautiful."

I felt chills all over my body. *She didn't say it was because she wanted to do their hair*, I thought. "Well, how are you going to make women feel beautiful?"

"By being a hairdresser."

"Or you could do something else," I suggested. "Like be an orthodontist."

"A what?"

"Somebody who makes people feel beautiful . . . by repairing their smiles."

Her eyes lit up.

I wasn't trying to throw her off course. I just wanted to inject that she had options to make people feel beautiful . . . if she wanted to.

My brother calls it "Lockjaw Syndrome." It's when we think about something and make up our minds that there aren't any alternatives to getting there. Man, I've learned that life will throw you all kinds of curve balls.

"You have a world of opportunities to live out making people feel beautiful," I told her. "Don't bet your future on one job title. Stay flexible while getting there. You're closer than you think."

The Five-Turn Fast Track Framework™—The Second Turn—Recalculate

The same goes for you, whether you work in fast food or make a six-figure salary. All you have to do is follow the **Five-Turn Fast Track Framework**™. It's time to set your new coordinates and listen for your second turn to **recalculate** from your current location in life, so you can see just how close your calling is. Just as I would've skipped the Fort Hood stop if I hadn't known we were less than an hour away, you can skip right over or drive further away from your calling. So pull over. Turn on your hazard lights. Take a good, honest look at where you currently are in your career—and begin to imagine how close you really are to where you've always wanted to be.

Sometimes, you need other people (just like I needed my wife, Josie) to recalculate for you. For example, a close friend told me their dream job was just one promotion away. Unfortunately, the job required more experience, education, and credentials than what they possessed.

"You may be closer than you think," I told my friend. "Go to your boss and ask, 'Are these requirements rigid? What does success in this department look like to you?' You want your boss to give you his or her definition of success so you can prove you may already have what it takes. Then follow up with, 'What if I told you I can help you get those results? I may not totally meet these listed requirements per se, but I offer equal, alternative qualifications. If I could help you get the results you're looking for, what would that look like to you?' And move forward from there."

My friend took my advice and landed a job interview. Today, he's living out his calling and doing what he loves—all because he was closer than he thought and he was willing to have that crucial conversation.

Remember your Gutsy Purpose Statement? It doesn't have to be a prophecy. It describes who you are meant to be and what you are meant to do *right now*.

After a meeting with my team, I chatted up one of our team members.

"You seemed disengaged a bit," I said.

"Yeah, I'm just thinking, man."

"Tell me, what would you rather be doing right now?"

"Me?" He glanced over his shoulder. "I'm doing what I love to do, Gerren."

"Stop it. You can be real with me."

"Well,"—he licked his lips—"I've always wanted to be a machinist."

"Yeah? What's so cool about that?"

"I love engines. Machines. Robots. I love taking them apart, seeing how they work, fixing them."

"How is *this* job helping you do that?"

"Um . . . *what?*"

"How is working here at Clean Slate helping you take things apart, see how they work, fix them, and so forth? What company do you know that needs someone like you, and have you reached out to them?"

"Nobody's gonna hire an old man like me!"

"*I* did."

"What do you mean?"

"Well," I said. I cleared my throat. *Teacher's mode, on.* "I'm looking at it this way—you *say* you want to be a machinist. But you actually love taking things apart and seeing what makes them work. I hired you because you're always early, you're dependable, and you do your job. I can afford to pay you what we currently pay you. But tell me. What other company out there is *dying* to find someone with your talents, dependability, and passion? Forget about the title! Who do you think is looking for you right now?"

He nodded, wheels turning.

"Have you ever thought to ask me what broken-down equipment we have that needs routine maintenance? Would that feed your machinist bug? Seriously. That would bring a *lot* of value to our company."

"I guess—I guess I never thought about that."

"There are opportunities where you can help us literally take things apart and see what makes them work. Then you improve them. Anything from process improvement to project management. See what I mean?"

"Process improvement. Project management," he repeated, enunciating like a guy trying to remember a lady's phone number. "Taking things apart and seeing what makes them work."

"Absolutely. Our job is our vehicle. Where do we want it to take us? Wherever that destination is, *we are closer than we think*."

You are closer than you think, too. It doesn't matter if you're at your first job or thinking about a second career after retirement. You have to be open to the bigger picture. If you lack a particular skill, at least you'll know what you need to reach your goal. It may only be "58 min." away. Like my machinist wannabe, make the most of this place—where you are right now. In his case, cleaning is simply a vehicle he can drive wherever he wants. Machine work is just another vehicle. So talk to your employer, your manager. Find out how you can bring value *right here*. You'll be surprised by what you find.

 Pump Your Brakes

You're where you need to be. So why do you need to be there? Maybe you hate what you're doing because you haven't figured out what your assignment is yet. What if you've become what you've always wanted to be when you grow up, but you just haven't realized it? It's not about where you are, it's about who you are when you're there.

I recently interviewed a lady who works for one of my vendors.

"I could be your mother, Gerren," Daisy said with a smile once we got started.

"Just tell me about yourself. Tell me what it is you enjoy doing. Tell me what you like."

"I like being compassionate, helpful, understanding. I once met a very frustrated customer, and now he's one of my best friends. Any time he calls to order, he asks for me. He even waits until I return to place an order."

"Who needs a compassionate, helpful, and understanding employee like you?"

"Any business, Gerren."

"Right. *Any* business could use those qualities. But which business do you *really* want to work for?"

"Nobody's ever asked me that question before. So I've never thought about it."

"Well, if every business needs your qualities, how can we find a business that can use these qualities to bring the most value possible? If you're compassionate, helpful, and useful, you could become an administrative assistant. But who really, *really* needs those qualities to make more sales? It could be a company that builds homes. A company that knows that when a customer comes through the door, it's imperative the first person they meet has a skill set like yours to ensure a sale happens. At a company like that, you'll earn more than you can imagine."

"I guess you're right. I think I have some homework to do."

"What are the top three things you enjoy doing personally? Because those are the things you'll do naturally in the work environment."

"I love making people smile," she said. "I just love it. I like to listen to someone and think of things that would be meaningful to them. So if they love donuts, I might be the person who surprises them with their favorite donut. Just seeing that smile cross their face makes me feel *so good*. I want to work with some cool people who love to do really cool things for each other. If I could do that, I don't think it would feel like a job."

"Can you find opportunities to do that within your company right now? If you can, you'll wake up every day *wanting* to do your job. And if you can add value to the company while doing it, they'll not only allow you to do it, they'll *pay* you to do it. I'll bet you're closer than you think. So what additional skills would you need to learn to be able to add that value in the company you work for right now?"

"Computers," Daisy said. "I don't do well with Excel. Microsoft Office, really. My boss wants to be able to give me a pile of stuff and say, 'Run with this.' But I like being trained one-on-one. Teach me what I need to know, and I'll learn it. But he just gives me the stuff and tells me to figure it out. That's why I'm looking for different work."

Her boss was a good friend of mine. If he understood how much Daisy *wanted* to bring value to the company, and where her skills gap was blocking the way, I knew he'd be happy to fill it—and he was. Just put yourself in an employer's shoes. If you haven't ever done that before, just take me. I'm owner and CEO of Clean Slate Janitorial. All the time, my clients' needs force me to grow in ways I once found scary. I'm one person with a small team. My employees have certain skills, but not all the skills (or the capacity) to help me grow how I want to just yet. Every day that passes, I feel more and more anxious about missed opportunities. Every time I visit my website, I wonder how many people I didn't convert.

I scour the net daily trying to find employee-productivity shortcuts. I've reached out to other companies and contractors for help. And I've met vendors I think of as vultures. "Sure, I can help you, Gerren. For a price," they squawk at me. They have sales quotas—I get it. But I'm only willing to invest in help that will give me confidence. No pressure. A confidant of sorts. A friend.

If I'm the smartest person in the room on all things, I'm in the wrong room. If I'm spending my time learning everything, I'm not spending my time setting and driving the vision. If I'm researching everything to build our company, I'm not employing and growing others. I need help.

If you're not a high-risk person who sets clear goals and accepts the weight of an organization's success or failure, don't come looking for a career at Clean Slate. I want to know from you where you might fit in at the company. What are you good at? Where do you want to showcase your skill set? I'll exchange value (a salary) for your gifts. The larger the problem you can help me solve, the more I'm willing to exchange for your wisdom, commitment, and delivery. I'll want to keep you close by, so I'll exchange more for that. In the meantime, I'm looking for new problems you can solve, because that helps you to grow as it does our company. It also increases your value. But wait! It's not just about you. There are other people here who want to grow also. Will you show them your wisdom? Will you help another as I've helped you? Can you multiply yourself? We all need help.

That's what every business owner thinks. So when was the last time you stopped and thought about how you could better use your skills inside their business at your current job? Identify what it is that you enjoy doing. What comes naturally? In what business, at what job, and in what industry would that be the most valuable? *That* is your destination. Your job is just the vehicle that takes you there. How close are you to that destination? Talk to your current employer and find out. Chances are, you're a lot closer than you think.

If you're an entrepreneur, working with your ideal client is your destination. Are you even targeting the right people with your advertising, marketing, and sales? If not, *update your GPS address*. If you're a student, go to the next career fair and speak with the hiring reps. Find your destination by interviewing *them*. You'll reach your one true calling a lot faster (and easier) if you start off near Nineveh than if you run away to Tarshish first.

No matter where you start, or how far into the journey you are, *every* person can recalculate their career path. Make the most of where you are right now—wherever that is. All you have to do is ask the right questions.

Key Point

Don't be surprised if you experience a flat tire at some point on your journey. It wasn't meant to hurt you. It happened so you could pull over and adjust your coordinates.

Action Steps

1. What have you been running away from that you know you were called to do?

2. What "storm" or flat tire have you recently experienced that was difficult for you?

3. Take a look at your coordinates (e.g., Your Gutsy Purpose Statement).

4. How close are you to experiencing it?

Chapter 4

Self-Promotion Isn't Selfish

"I guess you're wondering why I'm here," the kid seated across from me said. "What with the criminology degree and all."

"Yup. I am," I said. "But I'll tell you—it's not all that surprising. Some people never work in the field they studied."

"Really?"

"More people than you'd think."

"Okay, okay." He nodded. "The thing is, I love basketball. I played overseas. Professionally." He handed me a paper copy of his résumé, which I already had. "I want a flexible job so I can keep training, so I can make it in the league here."

"So why this job? Why Clean Slate?"

"Well, I love making things look neat. It's one of my strengths. I enjoy talking to people and working on teams. I'm good at setting things up, organizing, all that. Comes in handy on the court. But I need the flexibility and time so I can train for league tryouts."

"I like it when people know their own strengths and want to make them even stronger," I said. "That said, most employers would look at you and think, 'This guy isn't committed. He won't stay at a job long-term. I'd better turn him away.'"

The hope on his face faded. "I know. I know. I would think the same thing if I saw myself walk in the door. I just need a place to keep me going so I can go after my dreams. I'm pretty good. You should check out my highlight reel online."

"I'm not most employers."

His eyes brightened again.

"I appreciate your honesty. I don't think this third-shift office-cleaning position is for you. But you know what?" I let him hang for a second. "You'd be the *perfect* day porter. You would get to keep clients' environments neat and tidy, and you'd be talking with professionals all day long. You can use your natural abilities in an arena where you can be yourself *and* still focus on your goal."

"Wow. Yeah, that sounds great, Mr. Sprauve! When do I start?"

> **Pump Your Brakes**
> Even if what you're doing right now isn't what you want to do, if you do it with discipline, then it'll take you where you want to go.

How to Promote Yourself

A lot of people believe they have to wait around to be promoted. They try their hardest, go above and beyond at their job, and whisper a prayer that somebody—*anybody*—will notice. Most of the time, nobody does, and their hard work goes unrewarded. That's why I believe in *self-promotion*. I don't mean forcing yourself on people (when they're not interested) or telling the world how great you are (when you're not). Going around "selling" yourself like a door-to-door vacuum-cleaner salesperson practically *guarantees* nobody will buy what you're selling—much less promote you to the job of your dreams. When I say self-promotion, I mean driving your vehicle to your destination. Your calling. Your dream position on this journey. You already know you're closer than you think to your calling. Nothing is stopping you from hitting that turn signal, changing to the fast lane, and flying past traffic. My new day porter did that without even realizing it. He already had natural talents that, properly invested, could reap the reward of a good shot at professional basketball in America or abroad. All it took was a little creative thinking, a little questioning, and a *lot* of honesty to make working for me his vehicle and drive it closer to his one true calling.

But let's be real for a moment. Many times, decision makers and managers look at someone pursuing their calling and following their energy as overly ambitious. Impatient with the process. I believe that mind-set cripples people who seem ready.

A buddy of mine, Rolston Audain, called me one evening to check up and inquire how business was going. We hadn't spoken in over a year, but like childhood friends do, we picked up right where we left off. Two hours into the conversation he asked, "Gerren. Who on your team is probably bored with cleaning and may totally enjoy helping you grow your business in a different role?"

Although I'm someone who is all about growing others, I may have been missing these opportunities. So I said, "Thanks for the deep dive, Rolston. I'm going to take another look at my team. I don't believe I could possibly uncover it all through just a few intimate talks with them." If I missed it, and *I'm* open to this type of growth in people every day, I could only imagine how many decision makers out there don't care that much to even have the conversation! I was like Larry without even realizing it. *We hired you to do a job. Ugh!*

I don't care what your job is right now. You *can* shift that vehicle into high gear and accelerate toward your calling while everyone else sits back waiting for a promotion that may never come. It doesn't matter if the only job on your résumé is a part-time gig at Burger King. Maybe once or twice you stepped into a shift-management role. That is an *invaluable* strength. So your vehicle isn't *just* Burger King. It's an opportunity that, if you took full advantage of it, you could use to do *whatever you wanted*.

Stop for a second. No, really. Run through this exercise with me. Think about that one place where you worked, but you refuse to put it on your résumé because you're embarrassed or you believe it's not that meaningful. Write down the things you did well from the time you began getting ready for work until you clocked out.

- Did you schedule your alarm to ensure you would begin preparing to reach your appointment (your scheduled work time) on time?

- Did you iron your clothes the evening prior?

- Did you map out what bus routes you'd need to take and nailed everyone to get to work on time?

- Were you always cordial to the bus driver, Starbucks worker, garbage truck driver, etc.? Did you address customers by name?

- Did you bring in donuts?

- Were you instrumental in getting fifty customers in and out in an hour?

- Were the meals you prepared spot on, and was satisfaction written all over the customer's face?
- Were you consistent in the way you prepared things?
- Did you set up rooms well, all the time, every time?
- Were you the one who rarely called out sick?
- Did you take care of your health?
- Did you encourage others?
- Did you bring a smile to the workplace?
- Did you solve problems?
- Did you fix things?
- Did you make people return and ask for you?
- Did customers call you by name even when you didn't have a name tag?

I want you to think on the pettiest level. Why? Because all of those things you did well are examples of you exercising the muscles that would help you do bigger things well. Track the results of the day. How did you make life easier for your boss? Your coworkers? The customers? What problems did you take off their plate? Think nitty-gritty. Remember every time you added value. The question most employers have is, "Are you prepared to help me?"

Self-Promotion Isn't Selfish

If you've been working out those muscles, you're one step ahead of the game. The content, the industry, the level of expertise may be different, but the fact is you've been working out those muscles. Reaching the next level requires you now work a little harder at improving those things you do well. Not *did* well . . . *do well*. The motor is already on. The transmission is in gear. You're already moving. Just keep on moving. *Drive*.

The next time you step behind the counter register in your Burger King uniform, ask yourself, *Why am I here? What can I learn? What am I supposed to do with this experience?* You'll learn who else needs the skills you have, like that knack you have for managing people successfully. Who else out there needs that skill? Don't get caught up in titles like many do. Look at your skill set. See yourself based on who would benefit from your skill set. Do you motivate people? Do you help people be highly productive? Do you think fast to solve problems in a crisis?

Then, in your next interview, *promote yourself*. Go into that interview with the intention of helping that person grow their business—more customers, better customers, and increased value of products. Talk about the steps you took at Burger King to make some of those things happen. Trust me. You'll be setting yourself up for something better.

> **Pump Your Brakes**
> There is what you're hired to do, and there is what you accomplished while you were there. Maybe you got hired to flip burgers. But what were you able to do? You were part of the team that turned out how many burgers per hour. That's an accomplishment! Don't lie on your résumé, but make it clear how you went above and beyond for your employer. Yes, you did the job, but you lived. You created experiences that benefited everyone! When you share that in your interviews, the hiring manager gets to imagine how you'll "expand" beyond the job description to make a difference.

The Five-Turn Fast Track Framework™—The Third Turn—Drive

Of course, you can only self-promote properly if you actually take the time to invest in strengthening those skills. The Third Turn of the **Five-Turn Fast Track Framework™** is **Drive**. When you have an open road, stay in the fast lane. Don't be afraid to ask questions and strengthen your strengths—or to work on or leverage your weaknesses if they hold you back. Keep doing what you do well, and improve what you don't do well. Progress is that simple.

When I started Clean Slate Janitorial Services, I practiced the art of communicating every single day at my job. I was good, but I was not yet the *best* version of me. Whatever comes naturally to you, work on that strength every single day, no matter what car you're driving. Even if you work at Burger King, if you focus on the thing you do very well, you'll become the specialist. Not *a* specialist. *The* specialist.

Even today, I still invest in my skill set. Having employees and being a communicator, I can focus on perfecting my communication with my employees.

"How you guys doing? What do we need to do today? What do we need to work on? How you feeling? You're looking sharp, man! How can I help? What do you need from me?"

I'm bringing my strengths to the table and working on them every single day. I want you to do the same.

I hated reading when I was in high school. I hated reading when I was college. But something clicked when I got out of college. Now? I can't *stop* reading. I have books on my phone. I have books in my office. I have books at the house. Even when I'm taking a shower, I'm reading something. And I take multiple showers a day—just so I can read in the shower!

Sometimes when my team has a problem, I'll offer to come out and work alongside them. Some friends have asked me, "Why are you still working in the field?" When I work alone, I get to "read" my audiobooks. I get to determine how long I'm going to work, select a book, adjust how fast I want to listen, and press play! I enjoy those moments because that's when I get to dream, be encouraged, motivated, and problem solve, all while hearing my "friend" share a word with me. Have you ever needed your friend to share a good word with you, but they were unavailable? A good book fills in those gaps for me. Yeah, people think it's strange.

My mentee Kevin once asked me, "Gerren, why do you read so many books? How do you decide what book to read next?"

"I want to get better. Every day. So I ask myself, 'What stopped me today? What made me slow down? What can I be better at tomorrow?' These questions drive what book I read next. No complacency." I kept going before he could respond. "If something threw me for a loop today, I need to study up on that. Maybe I bombed a negotiation with a potential client. I gave in to their number, and I'm not profitable anymore. How can I negotiate better? I find a book, I learn, and I do better next time. Even if I'm moving forward, I read. I could be having a great day. But if I stop reading, I'm just sitting here in traffic idling. I'm burning gas and time. I don't want to just sit there. Gas is expensive! There's always going to be something challenging me and something moving me forward. The question is, how good do I want to be at that, and how soon? What do you want to get better at, Kevin?"

"Well, I never thought of that."

"If you don't want to get better, then you're just going to work, pay bills, work, pay bills."

"Huh."

"Reading matters. Because if you don't read, you hold yourself back from taking the next step."

"Huh," he said again.

I wasn't sure if he was paying attention. But I kept going. "Here's the deal. It's easy to complain. 'Why didn't I get that raise?' You know? Compare that to *investing* in yourself. Why not just pick up a book tonight and start studying how to get promoted? Can you think of any downsides to improving yourself?"

"Um, not really."

"Exactly! Say you ask for a raise but don't get it. You're still brighter. For you, not for your boss or anyone else. *For you*. So, wherever you end up going next, you can be a rockstar. You have the tools already. You're not waiting on anyone."

I don't know if Kevin ever took my advice. But *I* did. No matter how good or bad my day goes, I take the time to strengthen my strengths. I'm reading and learning more about what I really, *really* love—how to be a better communicator.

What do you do very well? Manage a schedule? Listen effectively? Do people walk away from you feeling good about themselves? Look for opportunities to do *more* of that wherever you are, and promote your ability to do it. Don't wait for somebody's approval. They're *your* talents, after all. Give yourself credit.

Another friend once said to me, "Gerren, your eyes are blinded. Life's hard. It's tough out there. Why do you have to be so positive all the time?"

All I could do was laugh. If I go on social media or read the news, and I look for the hate, I can find the hate. If I look for warm and uplifting stories, I can find them, too. I choose to look for the best in people. The world is already a Debbie Downer. You are what you seek. So seek the best in yourself, as well as in others.

When we identify who we are and why we're here, then we'll utilize our strengths on any assignment, in any vehicle that we're driving, and at any job that we have. If you're a great communicator like me, be a great communicator at your current job. If you negotiate, be a great negotiator. Your job is your assignment for right now. It's not the end. After this assignment, you'll get another one.

Most people don't do this. They never deviate from their job description and pay grade. In their heart, they may *know* what their calling is, but unless some promotion magically appears, they don't invest in it. They don't build up their natural strengths. They don't seek opportunities to promote themselves. It's like they're sitting on the side of the road. They learn nothing, and they go nowhere.

Cleaning was just a vehicle to get me in the door and engage my true strengths. I wanted to learn about my clients' businesses. I wanted to teach them how to create an environment that makes people want to return. I was more than their janitor—I was their *image consultant*. I took stress off their plate. I focused on how they presented themselves—not just how clean their space was—to the world. But I never would have been able to do that if I'd put my head down and never asked questions—if I'd never invested in my strengths.

If you want to drive to your calling *fast*, you have to get uncomfortable. Maybe you're the fastest car on the highway, but people in the slow lane try to cut you off or make obscene gestures at you. Haters don't matter, because haters don't get promoted. Noisy as they may be, haters are nothing to worry about.

When you're not cruising in high gear without a care in the world, showing off those natural strengths on the job, you may find yourself on the side of the road. With a flat tire. They happen. I would know. One Monday morning, my cleaning contractor dropped off the keys to every building we cleaned unexpectedly.

"I quit," she said. "I don't want to do this anymore with you. Best of luck, Gerren Sprauve."

It turns out she didn't have her crews clean all of my clients' offices that weekend. I had no idea until a shiny pile of keys plopped onto my desk. I didn't even have time to get upset. If you get a flat tire on the road to your calling, don't get upset. Don't expect someone else to fix your problems for you. I prayed softly, then sprang into action.

I solve big problems. I solve big problems. That's right, Gerren—you solve big problems. With that mentality, my heartbeat slowed down. I smiled as I reassured myself. I asked, *What do I need to do? Who do I need to call? Right. Call our clients.* I went through the list, starting with my major accounts.

"Gerren, it's okay. We'll be fine. Just come and take care of us once you get your cleaning crew all sorted out."

I had built such positive relationships over the years that not a single client fired me. All because I invested in them using my true strengths—communicating, teaching, mentoring, and serving. Isn't that what God teaches us to do? I am totally convinced that His hand was in it all.

Looking back, I thank that contractor for walking out on me because it allowed me to grow. I may not have liked how she did it, but maybe if it was done another way, we would've talked it out. But apparently it was time to buy a new pair of shoes. I was growing. Look at all your challenges as opportunities. Life is waiting for you. All the resources in the world and all the people in the world are willing and ready to help you grow. But they won't and can't help you until you've decided

Self-Promotion Isn't Selfish

to take on the challenges that life has to offer. I'm not the type of guy to look back and regret.

But . . . (I know, you saw that word coming.) I could've fast-tracked my calling years ago. I know when I worked in claims adjusting, I could've driven that vehicle all the way to my destiny. But I got a flat tire. And that time, it *was* my fault. I wasn't the most productive guy in the office. I tried to stay motivated, but everything around me was claims, claims, claims. I wasn't intentionally meeting new people. I wasn't having the conversations that would push me. I didn't know *how* to take advantage of the vehicle I was in. If I was to take what I've learned now back to my job in insurance, I would be one of the most promotable employees there. But I wasn't. I didn't know to show up early and prepare for my day. I was the guy who came home and complained, "Why can't I get everything done that I need to get done? There's just no extra time in the day." I would then walk around the house like a zombie and play video games before going to bed. What a spiral.

When I started Clean Slate, I realized that if I wanted to take Saturdays off, I couldn't afford unproductive habits. Most new entrepreneurs start working whenever and stop when they drop. So what did I do to keep from getting a flat? I bought productivity books. Productivity expert Brian Tracy wrote *Eat That Frog!*, a fun little book that teaches how to stop procrastinating and start getting more done in less time. That book taught me how to set great expectations and put benchmarks in place so that I can accomplish my goals. I get the most important work done first thing so that, no matter what else happens, I can feel accomplished at the end of the day.

My mistakes as a claims adjuster are now recycled into lessons for my employees. Now I teach them how to focus on the most important day-to-day tasks. I mentor them to set themselves up for success not just at Clean Slate, but over the course of their careers. That means I've got to set the example, and that's not always easy! If some hiccup occurs on the morning of the job, I may not get to my office until 3:00 p.m. I know I have to leave to pick up my daughters by 5:30. So I look at those two and a half hours and ask myself, *On the list of things I have to accomplish, what is the most important thing that I need to do today to get the best results?* And that is how I fill those two and a half hours.

It's kind of like going on vacation. Before you leave to go on vacation, do you know how much stuff you get done at home or on the job? You do *so* much work because you know you're going to be gone for a week and a half, and you don't want things snowballing.

I still have days when my patched tire rumbles on the pavement. I drag through my day, struggling to focus. Whether I just didn't start the day off well or something kicked me off course, I just have to get back into the rhythm. Once I see that happening, I call it a day. I just shut everything down. *Screw it.*

I'm going home. I take a drive to decompress, then go home to be with my family.

Sometimes, self-improvement isn't as obvious as reading a book. If you don't know how to change the flat tires on the highway to your calling, what do you do? *You ask.* At Clean Slate, we have a system that enables customers to leave raw, unedited feedback at any time. We also email or call the client directly after we've finished working at their facility. The client gets an opportunity to answer questions like, "Have we met your expectations? Have we exceeded your expectations? Or what are the ways we could improve?" In this way, we teach our clients how to measure our performance as *we* measure our performance. If we don't measure how we're doing, we'll never know if the customer is satisfied! If your GPS tells you to exit on the right in one hundred feet, but you're hanging out in the left lane, you'll never get where you want to go.

> **Pump Your Brakes**
>
> You want to do *this*. You want to do *that*. But you don't know how—or you can't follow through. Get help. You don't have to be great at everything. But what you're bad at will take you off the road. If you can't fix it yourself, find someone who can, and get their help. Your car needs all four wheels!

If you don't run your own business, you can still ask for feedback that helps you improve. My friend Anne works with teams across the world doing programming. Her typical meetings last *four hours.* In the long strings of code she writes, if she accidentally types two spaces instead of one, she could lose the company millions of dollars. And that's pretty much what happened.

"Gerren, I need you to talk me off the ledge." Anne called me one evening. "I think it's going to be one of those days."

"Tell me, what's the problem?" I asked her.

"Gerren, they're going to fire me."

"Oh, come on. No they're not. Your bosses love you."

She didn't say anything.

"Why would they fire you?" I asked.

"I screwed up. I *really* screwed up. Oh my goodness, I screwed up."

"Hold on—what happened?"

Anne explained the problems she was supposed to solve, what exactly she had done wrong, and how many people had been on the call. At the end she said, "I don't even know what I'm going to do."

"What's going to happen tonight?"

"I don't know. I don't think I'll get any sleep."

"What would help you sleep?"

"I have to tell them that I screwed up."

"Do you know how to tell them in a way that would fix the mistake?"

"No."

"Well, that's the most important thing to do right now. We need to figure out how you tell them about the mistake. Who do you know there who's screwed up before?"

"I don't know. Maybe . . . Tom."

"Okay. You call Tom and ask him how he responded to the team when he screwed up."

"Wow. Yeah. I guess I can do that."

"Anybody else?"

She laughed. "I don't think Jesus ever screwed up, but I'm gonna ask him."

"There's a smile. Prayer always helps."

When I got off the phone with Anne, she called Tom and got his advice. Then she mustered up the courage to talk to her boss and tell him she screwed up. Anne texted him just before midnight, *Do you have time for a phone call?*

He didn't respond to the text—he called. But Anne's boss didn't fire her. He didn't even discipline her. Instead, *he* offered suggestions to help.

"I believe the error happened because I had a double space," she explained to him on the phone. "I removed the double space, and then everything worked fine. I wanted you to know about this first, and I wanted to better understand how we can move forward."

"Okay," he replied. "Get an email together letting the rest of the team know that changes were made that we didn't anticipate affecting the other services due to a typo. If we get this information communicated sooner rather than later, we should be fine."

The next morning, Anne went to work and spoke to her boss's boss, a senior software architect.

"Okay," he said. "We can handle this. I want you to send me an email about the situation and tell every division involved everything that needs to be done. Then let's get a group together and test their machines. We'll communicate everything in a phone call later on today. That's how we're going to resolve the issue."

After Anne patched up the situation, she called to share the good news.

"I almost can't believe it, Gerren. Neither boss blamed me. They were all about moving forward. We put together a test group, which included senior management. We've created a channel we all communicate through so we know exactly what's taking place each time a test is done. That way everyone can provide their feedback, and this never happens again."

"How are you feeling about everything now?" I asked her.

Self-Promotion Isn't Selfish

"I feel better. I feel like I'm part of a team. Yesterday, when it was my issue and I hadn't told anyone about it, I felt dead. I felt like I was going to get fired. Now I'm working with individuals all around the organization to find a solution so it doesn't happen again. They're helping me put my best foot forward for other projects."

"Do you have any idea the wealth of information you just got over the past twelve hours?" I asked.

"What do you mean?"

"Dude! You just got a lesson from two different superiors telling you how to respond in a crisis. Do you know how valuable that is? You got your master's degree in handling a crisis, just like that. Just by focusing your energy on what's most important for tomorrow, versus worrying that they'd fire you."

Yes, Anne initially freaked out. She got upset. She didn't know how to change a flat. But she got advice and thought it through.

Am I going to pull onto the shoulder? Am I going to change lanes really quick? Or do I really need to slam my breaks? How's the person behind me? Are they paying attention?

Driving to your calling isn't always roses. Sometimes self-promotion means investing in your strengths and finding ways to put them to use. Other times, you need to get yourself out of the fast lane, change that flat tire, and recycle the rubber. In either case, self-promotion helps you better serve the world around you. And you better serve yourself, too.

Key Point

The way we solve problems is by influencing and maximizing our resources.

Action Steps

1. What do people tell you you're naturally good at? Delve into what you're good at. You'll naturally enjoy it. Go online and order books on that exact topic. They can even be audiobooks you listen to while you're doing whatever. Just go beyond good—be *best*. For example, I've got a knack for communicating, but I devour books on communication, negotiation, persuasion, and public speaking so I can *master* my strength. Know the art and science of what you're good at.

2. Do what you do best. Let others do what they do best. You both benefit.

3. Be known as the go-to specialist in your craft, not just another person out there who does what you do.

Chapter 5

It's Lonely Out Here

"I quit my job, Gerren," Nina said. "Since then, everything's been . . . okay."

"Just okay?" I asked.

"Yeah. My husband . . . you know how he is. Introvert. Old school mind-set. He's worked at the same place for what, twenty years now?"

"How does he feel about you starting your own consulting practice?"

"Worried." She shook her head. "But I understand. I was worried, too. I've taken a giant step into the unknown. But you know what's funny? Right after I quit, my previous boss left to take a job in Kansas City. And just like that, he became my first consulting client! I've helped him achieve the results he and his new company needed, and he's already moved up. It's been quite an experience so far."

"So you quit before he got his new position?"

"Yeah. And now here we are, working together again. He needs me for a new project. And get this, Gerren."

"Get what?"

"You remember when I quit, I told you I wasn't the only employee to leave?"

"Yeah, I remember."

"I started a new business partnership with the lady who quit along with me. It's official—I've charted a new course."

"Say what? Nina!" I hugged myself tightly, trying to contain my excitement. "Nina! Yo! That . . . is . . . awesome!" I grinned.

Nina could only laugh. "I know, Gerren. I know. We're doing it."

"Is she along for the ride?" I asked.

"Gerren, we complement each other. That's what's so amazing. Together, we balance out each other's strengths. We're going in the same direction. We make each other better consultants, better businesspeople, and better . . . well, *people*."

"You're basically carpooling then."

Nina laughed. "I guess you could call it that. We've got the same destination. Running a business is a lonely road, Gerren. You know that better than a lot of people."

"I sure do." I nodded. "I'm glad you found the carpool lane. No better place to be on the way to your destiny."

"I'm really enjoying this journey, Gerren. Thank you for sharing it with me. It seems we have similarities in several aspects of our lives. I will reflect on it all while on my flight tonight."

"I am extremely proud to call you my friend. I'm so glad God has put you on my path. I'm looking forward to remembering these conversations." Nina hurried away to accomplish some things before she left for Kansas City.

The Five-Turn Fast Track Framework™—The Fourth Turn—Carpool

We're not meant to go it alone in life. We humans are social beings. We're better together, and we're stronger, too. So why is it that so many people try to pursue their life's calling alone? Is it because we're afraid to ask for help? Because, deep down, we *know* we need it?

When I started Clean Slate Janitorial Services, I put on mental blinders. I didn't want detractors and naysayers getting in my head. After a month of pounding the pavement, jealousy got the better of me. I saw the UPS guy welcomed into that facility I'd just been thrown out of, and I wanted more than anything to be like that guy. You might say I "partnered" with that courier company to kick-start my lead generation. Whatever you call it, it worked!

That part-time delivery gig taught me a lesson that I remind myself of every single day: *Never go it alone*. We've all heard it said, "No man is an island." And yet we still fall trap to the mentality that no one can do it better than we can. I know I do on occasion. It's time we ditch that idea and live a life that shares the experiences.

That's why the fourth turn of the **Five-Turn Fast Track Framework**™ is **carpool**. If you and I had all the experience, the skills, and the wisdom we needed to find our callings, *we'd already be there*. Not a day goes by that I don't seek out some third-party expertise—whether to communicate more effectively or to mentor my employees so they promote themselves to bigger and better opportunities. That's what carpooling is all about. Out on the road, carpooling thins out the traffic so you don't get stuck in a jam. When you ride along with others headed in the same direction, you all get there quicker—and safer. If you don't see that pickup truck in your way when you try to change lanes, your passengers in the back seat just might. When you team up with people who have callings that complement yours, you help each other move quicker and you stay out of trouble.

Let me help you further. Maybe you're like me and you enjoy taking trips on the road with friends. What we do is we get as many into one vehicle comfortably and we ride out. With the kids safely strapped in and adults in the back to monitor any arguments, we set our destination on the GPS and go. To stay safe and on schedule, I'd have my designated wing person in the passenger seat who would be my additional eyes to move around traffic. I'd have someone in the rear who would watch for traffic when we're merging lanes. Another adult would be feeding the kids snacks and keeping them relatively quiet. I've got eyes everywhere, watching. It gives me confidence to focus on the destination.

Another thing we do when we're traveling in separate cars but going to the same destination is to get ahead and then slow down slightly to allow the other person in. We'll double tap the brakes in case there's traffic up ahead. We might be in separate cars, but we're watching out for each other. Granted there are some friends who do this well and others who are still learning how to effectively lead and follow.

I remember when my friends and I traveled to Washington, DC, for the inauguration of President Barack Obama. Eight adults with luggage. We thought about renting two minivans. The number-one question we all had in mind but didn't verbalize was, *What will we miss out on if we split up the group?* You know what I mean. The fun. The jokes. The conversation. It was a journey we all wanted to share. So what did we do? We pulled out bungee cords and tied all the luggage to the roof. Some of us sat on the floor in the aisle of the car, and together we carpooled. It was a phenomenal experience! One that we still joke about today.

That's what carpooling with the right people is like. It's phenomenal! On cold days, you'll share your winter gloves. When you've been standing too long, friends will allow you to lean on them. When you carpool, you meet unlikely people, and you strengthen relationships. You don't have to wait for the right people to find you. Ask! Look!

I run my business in a different kind of way. It's always giving back.

When I got started, and it was just me, a mop, and a bucket, I clearly remember all the people who took a chance on me. I made a bold move. I'm sure my wife sometimes looked at me sideways. *What did I sign up for again in this marriage?* My early residential clients, David and Connie, gave me a shot at cleaning their home. They were good to me! The day they shared with me their Wi-Fi, I was able to clean their home and begin to scale my business on a Friday. Fridays were long days, but I was always filled with gratitude while cleaning their home. I can't say it enough. The simple gift of Wi-Fi and a warm-hearted family meant I could be reached by potential clients and respond timely.

I tell you this because when I'm working with a new vendor or employee, I'm ever patient in my approach.

"Where are you now in your journey?" I might ask. "And what will working with us do for you?"

It's odd for the head of a company to care that much, but I want to know I'm carpooling with people who are in it for the entire journey, not just one block. Knowing that you're going somewhere with or without me is compelling. Knowing that you have a plan in place and you are actively working on your plan gives me the confidence to say, "Let's ride!" Or in the words of my buddy Darryl, "Hit it!"

> ### 🖊 Pump Your Brakes
> "I helped you as much as I could." Ever heard that from someone close to you? If their best is not good enough for you, it's time for that person to ride with someone else. Just because you're dropping them off at your next stop doesn't mean you're a bad person—or that you're meant to drive solo the next leg. But that seat does need to be free for when you come across the right person. The last thing you want is a car full of hitchhikers who don't know where they're supposed to go.

Clean Slate works very closely with another company, Tuxedo Impressions. The owner, Jamara Wilson, rides shotgun with me. We met at a Toastmasters event, where we've both trained to become poised and professional public speakers. I remember the first time I saw her introduce herself to the room like it was yesterday.

"I'm Jamara Wilson," she said confidently. "I own Tuxedo Impressions. We help small business owners become more efficient, standardize their operations, and improve their processes."

When the event wrapped, Jamara was at the top of my must-meet list.

"Excuse me. Jamara?" I called out to her as she was leaving. "Gerren Sprauve. I own Clean Slate Janitorial."

She smiled and accepted my handshake.

"Listen, I love what you said about getting efficient. I would love to meet with you to learn a little bit more about Tuxedo Impressions, what you're doing, how long you've been in business . . ."

"Sure," she said. "Absolutely."

We sat down and talked later that week. "I want to do business with you," I told her. "My processes could use some improvement! I'm running around putting out all of these fires. 'Gerren, we need this. Gerren, could you do that?' It's exhausting."

"That's exactly how most of my clients feel," she said, smiling. "We can turn that around."

"Listen, I don't know if I have enough business to hire you yet. It's just me and a few part-timers right now."

"Well, let's test it. Let's work together for a week and see how it goes. You send your organizational operations tasks over to us, and we'll knock them out for you."

We shook on it. The test was a success. Almost *too* much of a success. I'd send Jamara a task, and her team would knock it out and sent it right back. *I can't keep up with these people,* I thought. *Seriously.* It was like I'd been given a secret business-owner shortcut, but I couldn't keep the vehicle on the road. I got lost in the weeds of day-to-day tasks. At the time, I didn't know how to plan my day, much less plan to achieve my company's objectives and key results.

I need somebody else in this business. But who? I tossed and turned at night for a whole week trying to come up with an answer. And then a God thing happened. A friend and entrepreneur I'd grown up with stopped into town. George Brandy and I met for lunch, and I talked about my situation.

"No matter how fast I move, it's like I don't end up going anywhere," I said. "I know I'm on the right track, and Jamara's company is the asset I've been looking for. So what am I doing wrong?"

"Gerren, remember when I asked you, do you want to be self-employed, or do you want to run a business?"

"Yeah! I said that I wanted to run a business. Then I asked what the difference was."

"Well, there you go."

"You have to make some changes. You're more than a janitor—you're a consultant. But that means you own your own job. Your business is *all* you. You need to get a mentor. Somebody who was stuck in the day-to-day operations like you are, but they worked their way out and up to be the CEO."

"What kind of mentor?"

"A business coach."

After lunch, I went straight to my office and searched online for business coaches. If George thought I needed a coach in my vehicle, I'd find one. *I want to be the CEO. I need to be the CEO,* I thought. *I don't care how much coaching costs.* Then I saw the cost. *Oh. Wow. That's more than my car.*

I called Josie. "I want to try this coaching thing, like George said. But it's a really big investment. My biggest yet in the business. But remember when I started Clean Slate? We made it happen. I need your support. Do you think we can afford this?"

"I trust you, Gerren. Go for it."

God's Got It All Figured Out

That night, I narrowed down my potential search to one company I'd heard great things about. I prayed about the decision and reached out to them.

"We've got the right person to connect you with, Mr. Sprauve."

"Uh-huh."

I was so scared. *This person is going to think I'm an idiot. I don't know my business. I don't know my numbers. Ah hell!*

Gerren Sprauve, meet Eric Harmon.

"How much money do you want to make, Gerren?"

"I don't know. I'm less interested in money and more in how to build a sound business," I responded.

It's Lonely Out Here

"Well, you've won the lottery."

I was taken aback by Eric's response. *Kind of arrogant*, I thought. *I guess this is how coaches are. I'm about to be punked!*

I signed up to pay Eric for one hour's time every week. It wasn't chump change. With such an investment and a wife at home saying, "I trust you," I knew I had to put in the work—and I did. Eric gave me homework, and I tackled it. He told me to read books, and I busted them out. Some days I wouldn't complete as much as he expected and I would cross my fingers hoping we'd get through the call without him asking about it, but he never failed.

"How did you do with the homework, Gerren?"

Ugh!

Eric was very punctual. He was always the first person on the call. As our sixty minutes came to a close, we'd wrap up our call. But then I'd notice we'd go to eighty minutes, then ninety minutes. "Uh, Eric? We've gone over our scheduled time. I want to be respectful of your . . ."

"I'm well aware of the time, Gerren."

And he'd continue talking. Ninety minutes turned into two hours, then three. Every time I sent in my check, I wondered, "Am I taking advantage of our time?" Finally I just shut up and began digging in and becoming the best student I could be. The more I absorbed, the more Eric gave, week after week. Year after year!

I finally got the fortitude to stop him and ask, "Eric, why do you invest in me so much . . . for free?"

"Because you were looking for someone to learn from, and I always wanted someone to pour into."

To this very day those words still send paralyzing chills through my body. "God! Thank you!"

Eric often said, "Who would have thought it, Gerren? A white man from Utah connecting so deeply with a black man from the Virgin Islands."

He and I both knew why he said that. We'd talked about the differences between our race and our culture. But the common bond we shared—the love of learning, the respect for each other—trumped it all.

I had Eric in my life for four awesome and challenging years. He died suddenly from cancer. I mean, within a few months of finding out. It devastated me! His words (there were so many) to me were, "Gerren? I will only invest in you if you promise to invest in your community." (Insert paralyzing chills here again.)

Over the years, Eric and I got to work not *in* my business, but *on* my business. He helped me understand my role as the owner, how to add value to my clients and employees, and how to balance family responsibilities and business obligations without burning the candle at both ends. (Eric lived a life of burning the candles on both ends). Eric taught me how to make the most important transition—to go from self-employed to business owner. And it was all in my mind-set. Today, I find myself in conversations that the typical commercial cleaner wouldn't be having. It's not about the mop and the bucket—it's about solving business problems and creating exceptional experiences for clients, their employees, and their customers.

Meanwhile, with my focus on the big picture, Jamara helped me create processes *and* improve them. That changed everything. Out of the weeds and into the shortcut. For once in my lifetime, reading wasn't enough. I'd read and reread books. One in particular is called *The E-Myth: Why Small Businesses Don't Work and What to Do About It*. Another is *Profit First: Transform Your Business from a Cash-Eating Monster to a Money-Making Machine*. These books are phenomenal, but it was the people around me—and beside me in my vehicle—that made those lessons come to life.

When I started Clean Slate, I was a janitor. I did that very, very well. But I was more than a janitor, and I had gotten stuck. It's crazy how while choosing to go on this journey, I still fell victim to the trap. I was a manager. A manager of things, people, and processes. When I hired my first part-time employees, I had to teach them how to do what I already did very well. Teaching was part of my calling all along. But I couldn't handle all my different roles—business owner, salesperson, janitor, trainer. Without the support of Jamara and Eric, I probably wouldn't have made it to my one true calling. Not for a long while, at least. They were two of my biggest financial investments and two of my most successful business decisions.

I had more businesses callings than I was able to take on. Jamara and Eric helped me scale Clean Slate so I could seize those opportunities. I've gone from a guy wearing jeans and a polo shirt with sneakers to a gentleman in a suit and tie. People don't look at me and think, *Oh, that's just the cleaning guy* anymore. Now I step in the room, and they go, *He owns an image consulting business that specializes in janitorial solutions*. Investing in quality people in your life can help you drive toward your calling, too.

I've seen so many cleaning companies come and go over the years. All because their owners tried to go it alone. *I'll do everything myself—it's cheaper and I don't have to train anyone.* They retreat from management responsibilities into a technical position. *I'm happier when it's me and the bucket and mop anyway.*

These owners get stuck in the traffic of their daily tasks. Their businesses don't grow because they can't find the time to build them. We've all got just twenty-four hours in a day. We can only do so much work. When the clients call in, who's going to take care of them? Who's going to answer the phones? Who's going to do payroll? You can't do it all yourself. Not for long. Not if you value your sanity.

> **Pump Your Brakes**
> There is a difference between being alone and feeling lonely. Sometimes, everyone needs someone to talk to.

Whether you're an entrepreneur or a nine-to-five professional, there is a cost to opening up your vehicle to others. But if you reject advice, help, and support, you'll cost yourself way more down the line. On the road to your calling, you'll also pick up people who have *no business* being up in yours. You'll hear a rumble. It's not a flat tire—your trunk has a few stowaways! They snuck into your car at your last pit stop, and you'll have to kick them out.

I've had to release some of my friends. Not because I hate them. Not because they're bad people. They're just not the right influencers for me. I wish they could've come along with me so we could accomplish our dreams together. But not everybody wants that, and now that I think of it, it's probably the way it was supposed to be.

"Dude, mind your own business," I've had to lovingly tell former friends. "Jump on your own journey. Focus on you and your family. Just take care of them, and the rest will work out."

It's better to ride alone than let back-seat drivers steer you off course. Still, carpooling isn't all about you. Just like with Nina, you don't want somebody who's just along for the ride. And that other person didn't hire *you* to be their chauffeur. Add value to each other. How can you help each other on the highway to your callings?

In the first week of Clean Slate, I didn't have any answers. I looked around town, seeking out people. *Where should I go to market myself? How can I get and keep that first client?* I went to networking groups. I tried to ask other business owners for advice, but they hoarded their information. They weren't interested in carpooling. That's the way it goes sometimes. Their loss. My past experience behooves me to encourage and support others. I support my family, my employees, and my clients. Even if I don't get anything out of it, I invest in other people's futures. When you meet people on the road who complement your calling, *invest*! Invite them into your vehicle, and program the GPS together. If you are strong where they are weak, and they are weak where you are strong, even better! You could become each other's greatest asset. If it doesn't work out, kick them out at the next pit stop. But if you find the right passengers to carpool with, not only will you end up at your destination together, but you'll get there faster than you ever thought possible.

And you won't have to go it alone.

Key Point

If you're awesome at what you do, and I'm awesome at what I do, we may need each other at some point. If and when we're both in need, guess who we're going to call?

Action Steps

1. When you carpool, look for people who are smarter than you.

2. Look for people whose abilities intimidate you a little bit, but they're crazy supportive of those around them. They care more about your success than their ego.

3. Look for people who complement anyone else in your vehicle.

4. Vet everyone you're thinking about allowing inside that vehicle. Ask:

    - Where are you now?

    - Where are you going?

    - How fast do you drive?

    - Can I trust your driving?

    - Is our vehicle big enough for everyone?

Chapter 6

You Have Arrived

"Take a seat, Gerren," my client said. He and his business partner sat across from me at the conference-room table. "We need to . . . uh . . . *talk*."

It was 2009. The economy was going down. But I had no clue. The office was unusually quiet. When I would come to clean that building at the close of business, I'd always arrive early to greet employees leaving for the day. Not today. The place was a ghost town.

"Sure. Talk to me," I said. I took off my rubber gloves, shook both their hands, and sat down.

"Well, Gerren . . ." The other co-owner folded his hands on the table. "Business is hurting right now. I don't know if you've been seeing the headlines about the housing market going down."

"Honestly, I've been laser focused on my clients. Same as you guys, I'm sure. Pursuing new accounts and doing what we at Clean Slate do well."

"That's good, Gerren, for you. But to be frank, the economy is crashing. Our biggest account let us go over the weekend," my client said. "We have to . . . uh, downsize. Get reasonable with operational expenditures. Like payroll and such."

I swallowed hard. "Are you thinking of letting Clean Slate go soon?"

"No, not"—his partner rubbed his face in his hands—"not exactly. What we're trying to say is, we *did* downsize. We literally laid off all of our employees this morning. All of them."

"Except contractors," my client said. "And you're the only contractor we have. While we try to sort things out and recover, we can't afford to let prospects meet with the two of us in an office that looks like a dump."

"So it's just us now," his partner said. "For the time being."

"I don't get it. Then why keep me on? There won't be much to clean now with nobody here. A lot of empty desks."

"The thing is, Gerren, every day you come in here you're always asking these questions that push us to think differently. Even though you're the cleaning guy. I mean, you're *more* than a cleaning guy, obviously. All the times we've bounced ideas off you? It's like you're a one-man advisory board."

"I . . . don't know what to say. I'm flattered. I'm still learning so much. But it's clear you've hit a rough patch. Tough times and stuff. What I love is seeing my clients thrive. So what I'm trying to say is"—I swallowed again—"Why not let me scale down my services for you?"

Both partners shook their heads at me.

"Hold on," I said. "As opposed to cleaning for you five days a week, how about I come in three? Save a little money with me, and maybe you can put it toward paying another person."

"We'll consider it. I mean, that—that's a brave offer. You don't have to cut into our agreement."

"Look, if there's a way I can help your business stay afloat so you'll still be around for the people depending on you, I'm going to do that. I can always find another client. But all of those people who depend on you to stay in business—employees, vendors, their families—I think they're all more important than me just keeping a client." I paused. They waited for more. "The way I see it, I've arrived. I'm doing what I love. Adding value to business owners like you, just like you said. Now it's time for me to help others."

> **Pump Your Brakes**
> Acts of service are acts of service. It doesn't matter if you're cleaning someone's building or helping them make the right decision at a crossroads. If you can serve, you probably should. If you can help, why not help?

What Happens When You Find "It"

I hate when people call themselves self-made millionaires. "I hustled my way to success all by myself!" they say. *No, you didn't. Wrong. Someone paved that road for you long before you found it.* It's a deal-breaker for me. If you won't help others, if you don't give part of yourself, if you don't offer to help out, or if you say it's not part of your job, you can't work with me. I don't even want you around. This especially applies to people like me who are fortunate enough to have "arrived." You've reached your destination. You're doing what you were *made* to do. If that's the case, then don't think twice. Let your joy flow through you and into everyone you meet. You have a gift, and you're meant to share it. If you've arrived, make the most of your destination.

When I found myself coaching, mentoring, and teaching business owners, I knew that was "it." Even as a janitor cleaning toilets. But I had more gifts than just moving a mop and bucket around an office. And I didn't keep them to myself. I shared them. And as the owner of Clean Slate, I moved up in people's minds from their janitor to their consultant.

Arriving at your calling isn't about having bigger pockets. It's about having an abundance of joy because you're doing what you know God created you to do, regardless of career, job description, or even salary. In fact, my little stunt to save my clients money almost broke *my* business.

A couple of years ago, Josie and I read through some old bank statements we no longer needed and were about to shred.

"Yo, Josie! Come see this!" I called out from the living room. "Did you know about this?"

"What? Know about what? What is it?"

"A 2009 bank statement. It's the checking account balance for Clean Slate." I read off the number. "*Negative one hundred dollars, eighty-six cents.*"

"Seriously?"

"Dead seriously. Did you realize how broke we were back then?"

We dug through and found statements after statements of not-so-flattering balances.

"Let me see that." I handed her the statement. "Huh."

Josie smiled and nodded. "Yes, Gerren. This really was us, but I trusted you."

Ugh! My wife! I love this woman. Talk about having the right people in your corner.

"We never worried about us," I said. "We just kept focusing on taking care of our clients and helping them look their best. Even if we can't sell Clean Slate to cash out and retire, it's still been worth it. I've still been able to be a teacher, mentor, coach on this wild journey. Thank you."

I believe what I told Josie today as much as ever. My business is just a vehicle. I can't tie my self-worth to my net worth. My calling is all about adding value. Through Clean Slate, I helped several business owners weather the recession. I offered several of my own employees their first full-time jobs. For many of them, that job made it possible for them to buy their first new car or move from an apartment to their very own house or go to college.

Your calling doesn't just exist to make you happy. It exists to make the world around you a better place. Hoard your gifts, and you'll suck the life out of everyone around you—including *you*. In the New Testament, Jesus tells a parable about a businessman who entrusts his servants to invest his wealth. In the end, the businessman didn't care *how much* return his servants got from their investments. He celebrated those who got *a* return on investment. He only punished the servant who kept the money to himself, worried that he'd lose it.

My business coach, Eric Harmon, reminded me of that parable when I hired him. "Promise me one thing,

Gerren," he said on our first official call. "Promise me that if I invest in you, you'll invest in others. Remember, givers gain."

"I promise."

Every day, I do whatever it takes to fulfill that promise. The other day, I decided to open the door for anyone I saw near a door. It doesn't get any simpler than that! At the end of the day, I might not have felt accomplished at work, but I did make life a little bit happier for everyone with whom I came in contact. Serving others through your calling doesn't have to be as grand as helping a business in an economic downturn—much less the worst one of our generation. It's as simple as opening the door for someone if you get there first.

> **Pump Your Brakes**
> Everybody needs balance between giving of yourself to the world and giving of yourself to those closest to you. Yes, you can make an impact on the world, but remember who makes your day—don't forget about their needs!

The Five-Turn Fast Track Framework™—The Fifth Turn—Arrive

That's what arrival is all about. When you **arrive**—the fifth and final turn of the **Five-Turn Fast Track Framework**™—any success you achieve should not be all about you. Celebrate, of course. Feel the joy and the gratitude, then let the overflow benefit everyone around you. Help people get started doing what they struggle with if it comes easily to you. Remember, there's someone out there trying to get to mile marker fifty, and you're already putting your car in park. Look around for people who look lost, and offer to give them directions. After all, most people don't like to ask for directions! They're too ashamed. But they *do* want help. You can say, "I know you don't want to ask for help. But if you need it, I'm here."

I like to work an offer of help into my elevator pitch. When I ask questions in an interview like, "What's your biggest challenge? What will help you? What's holding you back? What problems can I help you solve?" I benefit just as much as the person I'm asking.

Even when I'm out growing my business, I'm focused on giving back. At networking events, I always bring seven business cards. I only intend to use three, but seven is a nice number. Why only three? Because within the average hour-and-a-half-long networking event, I'm looking only for genuine conversation. I don't go bouncing around the room, handing out cards to everyone I meet. Too many businesspeople swarm the room and pass out business cards, flyers, pamphlets—all without ever introducing themselves or even making eye contact!

People love to talk about themselves, so that's exactly what I let them do. After all, 90 percent of good communication is listening. I enjoy listening to people, understanding their needs, and helping them find a solution. Through studying the art of communication, I've made myself better at offering solutions they'll say yes to. I never really *try* to sell anything, but more often than not, I walk out of networking events with appointments—and clients.

Of course, I don't always have all the answers. When I meet someone with a problem I don't know how to fix, I *find* the answers so I can lead them in the right direction. Even if that person never becomes a client, I become a resource for them—a point of contact. Ninety percent of the time, they end up referring me to business owners and property managers who *do* become my clients. It turns out, sharing your talents is almost always profitable in one way or another. You can find ways to share your talents no matter where you are. If you have an entry-level sales job and your calling is helping people solve everyday problems, congratulations! As the GPS says, "You have arrived." Now make the most of your destination to provide value to others and, in turn, yourself.

But, Gerren! you're thinking. *How in the world does a minimum-wage commission sales job mean I've "arrived"? Is that really my "calling"?*

Let me ask you something. If I drive to Walt Disney World, park my car in the lot, and sit there baking in the heat, guess what? All I'd see around me are cars and asphalt and whatever heatstroke makes me hallucinate. *Really? This is Disney World? That's it? How in the world does a parking lot constitute "the happiest place on earth"?*

You see my point. So get out of your car! I'm talking about exploring your destination, and in turn, your calling. Break out of your usual routine. Discover the possibilities to make the world—and *your* world—a much better place. And if you're doing what comes naturally, you'll find there are people out there who need what you have to offer. In many cases, they'll reward you handsomely for it.

Last year, I walked into my local shoe store looking for a new pair of work shoes. The second I made it past the entrance, the clerk came up to me and smiled.

"What brings you in today, sir?"

"Listen, my feet are killing me. In my business, I walk a lot. These"—I pointed down at my dress shoes—"aren't doing it for me."

"All right, what would you like to do about it?"

"Well, I need my feet to not kill me anymore, for one thing!"

"Okay, let's get to the root of your problem."

You're speaking my language, pal! I thought.

"So you walk often and stand on your feet a lot?" He walked me to the athletic aisle. "Do you run as well?"

I answered his questions, and he picked out three pairs for me to try. After trying on the first two, I slipped into the last pair—beautiful red Brooks. I walked around the store and fell in love.

"Just throw those away, would you?" I said of the pair I'd worn into the store. "I'll wear these out."

That clerk helped me solve my problem, and my feet have been happy ever since. Get this. I'm not a flashy guy, so red sneakers weren't really what I wanted. I'd never worn or known about the Brooks brand, but they felt so darn good on my feet. I asked for his business card, and I emailed him a thank-you note for helping me select the right pair of shoes. The next job he applies for, he can bring a printed copy of that email with his résumé. I can think of about a dozen different businesses off the top of my head who need a strong salesperson like him. Oh, and roughly half of those jobs have a six-figure earning potential. Going out of your way to help someone when it's not required goes a long way.

I bet people are waiting for your skills, too. I don't necessarily mean you should give your two weeks' notice right now. But somebody out there wants what you have to offer. People are waiting for you to show up and present a prepared version of you. Sounds a little too simple, doesn't it? Fair enough. But you've *already* arrived, remember? You know your purpose. You're in the zone. Now it's time to find other people, help them find *their* zone, and celebrate together. Sometimes, that's as easy as a single conversation.

I boarded a mostly empty flight back to Florida. The business conference I'd attended in Wisconsin wrapped two hours before departure, and I was still pretty wired from the conversations I'd had. On that particular airline, you could choose your own seat, so I did—next to a couple and their two daughters occupying a whole row.

"Do you mind if I sit here with you guys?"

"Sure, go ahead." The woman smiled. "Sit."

I took a seat next to her and her husband and opened an e-book on my smartphone. We kept to ourselves until we got into the air. Once the ride smoothed out, I turned to the woman.

"I'd like to ask you a question. It's an odd question. But I'm interested in your response."

"Go ahead." She looked pleased as she looked up from her novel. "Anything to pass the flight time, right?"

"When you look at carpets in your home, what comes to your mind?"

She tilted her head. "Huh?"

"I *did* say it was an odd question."

"Oh, right. Well, I guess I want my carpets to look brand new. I want them to feel soft and warm. With the kids and our dogs and cats . . . well, they run through it so much that there's a traffic lane all through the carpets."

You Have Arrived

"Okay. And what do you think about that traffic lane?"

"Honestly, I feel embarrassed when people come over. The carpets are white, I mean, they *were* white, so every stain shows. Plus, the kids, the dogs, all that hair. *Ugh*."

I took mental notes as she talked. I might be able to give her some free tips to help her keep her carpets clean, but here she is helping *me*. Later, I wrote down the key phrases she used to describe how she—the average consumer—thinks about her carpets at home. I wouldn't know what to say in a residential cleaning brochure otherwise.

"Why do you ask?" she said. "Are you a carpet cleaner or something?"

"Actually, yes, that's part of what I do. Gerren Sprauve, CEO of Clean Slate Janitorial Services. We're image consultants who specialize in commercial janitorial services. The plan is to eventually add a residential wing back into the business."

"Really? Are you in Wisconsin? Can you come to my home and clean our carpets?"

"Orlando, actually. I'm heading home from a business conference. But let me tell you, there's this great carpet-cleaning machine you can get."

"Can I buy one through you to make sure you get a kickback?"

Here I am, just giving this lady a small cleaning tip, and she's trying to throw her money at me! Adding value really does pay off. That's the thing about business. People think it's about a website, fancy business cards, or a résumé you have your graphic designer buddy create. Success is really about helping people think through their problems. If you take the time to be curious about the people that you come in contact with, you'll always be employable. Honestly, even as a CEO, I don't know how to "get clients." But I do know how to help people, and that's more than enough to keep me booked. Show up prepared to help, and the hard work is done.

I met several business start-up owners at that conference. I traveled the start-up road so long ago, and I arrived at the destination we all want—business success. So I knew the questions they had on their minds. But because I was just an attendee, not a keynote speaker, I couldn't answer those start-up-stage questions. So during the Q&A, *I* asked them.

At lunch, a young couple came up to me and introduced themselves. "You asked the best questions," the wife said. "As soon as you started talking, we were like, 'That's exactly what we were thinking!' We just didn't know how to phrase the questions. So thank you."

The husband thanked me, too, shook my hand, and pointed to my tablet. "I see that you're recording everything. Do you mind sharing it with us when we get back to Idaho?"

"Sure," I said. "I'll upload all the videos online and send the links to you. Then you'll have all the training you need for your business."

"Actually, could we set up a call with you? You've obviously done this whole starting and growing a business thing, and—"

"Absolutely. I'd be glad to."

And we did. Did I invoice the couple for my start-up advice? Nope. I could have, and they would've paid, too. But I made a promise to Eric and to myself. *When you arrive, suddenly, the world's not about you anymore.*

Think about yourself. Think about your tomorrow. What can you do to be a rock at your place of business? At your church? In your family? You don't have to be an entrepreneur to get ahead, savor success, and give back. What's stopping you from investing your talents right where you are?

When I speak at colleges and universities, I remind students not to hang out, chill, and forget about their grades. Don't be like me and learn that lesson the hard way. Because here's the deal. One day, you're going to tell your life story to your kids or your grandkids. What example will you have set? Will they think, *Huh, I guess that's all there is to life*, or will they say, "Wow, I can be whatever I want to be as long as I help other people"?

When you arrive at your destination, share the lessons you learned with the world. Thank those who paved the way for you by paving the way for others. Help others find their calling, and that kindness will come back to you tenfold. So what are you waiting for? It's as easy as asking the right questions, shutting up, and letting people find their own way.

You don't even have to be at your destination to help others out. No matter where you are, *you're still ahead of someone else*. Here's what I mean. Have you ever heard anyone say, "I've been working here for all of these years, and they haven't given me a raise"? I have. And before I chime along with them and agree, I pause to ask a few questions.

- How are you as an employee?
- Are you working to be the best version of you?
- What are you known for in the office?
- If I were to call your name, what would other people tell me about you?
- Other than "working hard," what skills do you need to have to get the kind of money you're looking for? Where are you in that process?
- Do you understand the challenges the position deals with, and are you prepared to deliver on the results needed?

- If you are, is that what you're known for? Delivering on results?

When I take people down this road, they see how close (or far) they are to deserving that raise and promotion. Granted, not everyone gets an opportunity at their current place of employment to be the best version of themselves. But that doesn't mean there isn't another company out there in need of those skills. Were you able to gain new skills or practice using existing ones as a result of working at that place where you didn't get the promotion? If so, chances are that's what that job was supposed to give you. It probably wasn't supposed to be your end-all-be-all. They didn't allow you to get comfortable, because you've got places to go.

So where to next? We're all on this journey. We're all going places. From city to city helping, serving, teaching, and giving. Who said that where you are is where you're to be until you retire? You've grown, remember? You're changing. And there are people, circumstances, and conditions in need of your new knowledge.

Sometimes we work so hard to focus on the things of least importance. We feel like we don't have anything to offer. Every time I come upon traffic on a particular highway in my city of Orlando, Florida, I reach out to my Orlando family and let them know to avoid this highway.

The quick heads-up allows anyone who was planning to get to their appointment the opportunity to take a different route. What difference does two miles make? Two exits? *Whew! Thank you. Had I passed this last exit, I would've been in the traffic you're in . . . and late!*

You may think you're of no value to the world, but the fact is, if you're just two miles ahead, you can provide the right people with valuable information that could change their course. You're that powerful! Many times, unfortunately, we just get upset about the traffic and never think about our contribution to others.

Yeah, I get it. You want that promotion. You want to get to your destination. Who did you help along the way, though? I've always found that when I get myself into a helpful state, I bring different energy to the room, to work, to my team. I'm better able to understand more complex issues and challenges because my awareness is different. I'm not *me* focused, but *you* focused.

That opened me up to all sorts of opportunities that would've passed me by. I want to help you open up your awareness, too, so you'll realize that life isn't doing anything *to* you, but *for* you. Yes, there are certain people, certain demographics who may feel they always seem to get the short end of the stick. That's a question I'll take up with Jesus when I make it to heaven. For now, the question I ask myself is, *What's the downside to getting better?*

Ask yourself the same. And remember the Two Miles Ahead analogy. You can help *anyone* who is behind you on the highway of life—and be of great value. You just have to be willing and be open to caring for those sharing the road with you.

Key Point

Your calling comes alive when you learn and then share what you've learned with others. That's what matters the most—not your salary, not your status, not your success.

Action Steps

1. Look around. Find someone who needs what you know. What little you think you know may be the missing wisdom another person needs to succeed.

2. Ask the person, "What's holding you back?" If you don't share what helps people take that first step, you're not helping; you're just giving information.

3. People don't like to be told what to do. Don't give away the answer. Help the person find the answer for themselves. Draw it out of them. Help them find their way. Say, "Tell me about what you want. What have you tried so far? Have you considered this? What do you think would happen if you did? What should you do next?"

Chapter 7

Fast Track for Everyone

I'd just gotten back to my office from a training on public speaking with my nephew, Deonte'. Traffic had put us back a few minutes. My afternoon appointment, a potential employee, waited in the lobby. I apologized.

"I'm so sorry to make you wait. Can you give me sixty seconds? Just come on back in about a minute."

Deonte' followed me on the short walk back to my office. "Uncle Gerren, do you want me to go wait in the lobby or . . ."

"Actually,"—I thought for a moment—"you know the stuff we just learned about nonverbal communication and body language?"

"Yeah."

"Well, that guy out there is going to come back for an interview, and I think I want you to talk to him with me."

"You mean—you mean you want me to help you interview him?"

"Yes, I do. I want you to pay attention to his body language and tell me what you think."

"Cool! I can do that."

My nephew was thirteen at the time.

Moments later, the candidate—John—knocked lightly on the doorframe of my office. "Is now a good time to come back?"

"Sure! Come on in. Gerren Sprauve, CEO, Clean Slate Janitorial," I formally introduced myself. "And this is my business partner, Deonte' George." I winked at my nephew.

"Uh . . . okay. All right." John gave me the side eye. "How are you?"

Deonte' fell right into character. "I'm well. It's a pleasure to meet you, sir." He shook John's hand and took a seat next to him.

"So tell me why you're here," I said. "What about Clean Slate interests you? What are you looking for?"

"Well, I saw the post that you all were hiring for a day porter, and I'm looking for good, steady, work." He stirred. "So, yeah."

"Interesting." I swiveled my chair to face my nephew. "Deonte', do you have any questions for this gentleman?"

"Yes. I do." Deonte' nodded once. "What value do you feel you can bring to our organization?"

John chuckled. "You'll have to excuse me, but I've got to shake your hand again, man. No one has ever asked me a question like that before."

Deonte' accepted his second handshake. "Go on."

I quietly slipped my phone out of my pocket, opened my camera app, and hit "Record." All out of view, of course.

"I feel I have a great attitude," John said. "I can walk into the workplace, and if people are feeling down, I can lift them up."

"I see. I see," my nephew said. "Anything else you want to add?"

"Um, I don't think so." He shot me a look that seemed to say, *Help me!*

I kept a straight face. "Deonte', do you have any other questions right now?"

"Not right now, Uncle. You can take it from here."

John smiled. Probably out of relief.

"John, have you ever heard of what's called a 'unique selling proposition'?"

"Yeah, I've heard of it, but I couldn't exactly tell you what it is. Why do you ask?"

"Fair enough. It's basically what you, as a business, offer customers that no one else does. That's all well and good, but at Clean Slate, we have a unique selling *promise*." Deonte' *mm-hmmed* an affirmation. "Our promise is to create an experience so great, you'll feel the need to tell your friends. That's what we do. The Clean Slate experience is one that is clean, fresh, and inviting. That's our promise. Each and every day we come into a facility, it's to create a clean, fresh, and inviting environment. Clients look at us and say, 'Wow, that's what we need around here.'"

John nodded. "Okay, okay. I can see myself helping you deliver on that."

I kicked it back to Deonte'. "Can you explain to John how we create clean, fresh, inviting environments and why our performance is so important?" Deonte' had ridden along with me on jobs for several years. He knew the business inside and out.

"Typically, we get to work fifteen minutes early. We get there early because we want to be settled, not rushing around and sweating, coming into the office. Is that something you can handle?"

"Yeah, I mean, I always made sure to show up early at my last job. Won't be a problem here," John said.

"Very good," Deonte' said. "You may feel intimidated by all these questions." *You're killing me here, kid!* "Now, I noticed that you have a tattoo on your arm. If you were to work for us, we'd probably ask you to wear a long-sleeved shirt. Some people might look at your tattoo and wonder, 'Is this guy a thug?'"

I'd never seen a grown man look more embarrassed.

"Don't get me wrong, John," Deonte' cruised on, "we don't think you're a thug. You might have a great personality. But our clients don't know that. As you know, we're hiring for a day-porter position. If you're going to be a day porter, your job is to represent not only our company, but theirs. You also represent your personal brand. It always takes some time for our clients to get accustomed to new day porters, so you'll be expected to wear a uniform."

"All of this is important to know." I intercepted the conversation before this little dude had John in tears. "But just as importantly, we need to know if *we* are the right fit for *you*. So I want to ask you what you want out of this job. And by that I mean, what do you hope to achieve in your life *because* you got this job?"

"What I want out of this job . . ." I could see John dreaming behind his eyes. "Well, to be honest, I need a car. I want to go back to school. I'm trying to save up so I can go back and major in performing arts."

I started writing on my notepad. "If you don't have a car, would the bus get you to school? I mean, is that how you got here today?"

"Well, right, but I could get to school quicker with a car."

"I get that, but your primary goal is to go back to school, right?"

"Yes." He nodded.

"So if it took you a little while to save up for a car, you could still go ahead and start school, right?

"Well, yeah. Yes, I could."

"Great." I jotted down a couple more notes.

"Are you—" He leaned over the desk. "Are you writing down my goals?"

"Of course. I'm jotting down the things you said were important to you. What's the point of you coming to work here if your goals aren't clear? If you have that, you can then decide on your plan to accomplish them. I know if hired, you probably won't work here forever. Let's at least be looking in the same direction."

John leaned back in his chair. "Wow. I like you. I like you both. And I like . . . whatever *this* is."

We spoke a bit more before I tore the page off my pad and handed John the notes. "Here's the plan you just told me that will get you back to school. Now it's your turn. You work your plan. Whether you work with us or for someone else, work your plan. Sometimes, we have so much going around and around in our heads. We think we know what we want. But if you don't write it down, it's only a passing thought. Just press 'Play.' Work the plan, and the plan works for you." I stood up. "Thanks for coming in today. Either way, we'll call you within two weeks."

"I . . . thank you. Listen, before I go, I have to tell you—this didn't feel like an interview at all to me. This felt like a mentorship program."

"It is. That's what we do," I said.

"I've never experienced anything like this before." John shook my hand and then my nephew's. "And I don't know how old you are, but you're going places." Then he walked out. I turned off my camera.

"Well? How'd that go?" Deonte' turned back into my thirteen-year-old nephew. "You like that part about me being your business partner? He ate that up! I could tell from his body language!"

"You blew my mind, little dude." I gave him a high five. "Everything I've been sharing with you over the years, and today you remembered all of it. I'm proud of you." I gave him a few bucks to back up my praise. "Now go get something for yourself from the vending machine."

🏁 Pump Your Brakes

Set aside the fear of messing up. When you give someone the opportunity to mess up, everyone gets to learn something. When they mess up, you get to see how good—and bad—they really are. They do, too. You can only pass the tests you're allowed to take.

So You Found Your Calling. Do This Next.

Most employers, supervisors, and managers don't give their employees the opportunity to try to do something amazing. The same goes for many teachers, instructors, and professors. (My mother was an educator, and she could tell you some stories!) They just expect people to already know what to do. *It's up to you to prepare ahead of time. It's part of the job. Figure it out.* I believe in just the opposite. That's why I've dedicated my life and my business to mentoring people. Everyone who comes into Clean Slate gets mentored. Everyone. I don't care if you're a seven-figure business owner or a weekend-day-porter job candidate.

Or a thirteen-year-old kid. If I hadn't let Deonte' in on that interview, he wouldn't have gotten the chance to implement everything he'd learned. I gave him the opportunity to apply his knowledge and natural abilities, and he really got to shine. The truth of the matter is, that's what *real* leaders do. We help people grow. We serve them. And we do whatever we can to help them identify, reach, and make the most of their destiny. I created The Five-Turn Fast-Track Framework™ not only so *you* can experience the joy living life according to your true purpose, but so you could help those below you do so, too. Now, by "below," I don't mean that they're *beneath* you. I'm talking about the people you're responsible for and accountable to. Employees. Students. Interns. Your congregation. Your team. Your tribe.

We've all had bosses who hate people. They got promoted based on tenure, nepotism, or familiarity with the department in question. They treat you like it's their job to tell you what to do, and that's it. But that's not how Jesus rolled. His ministry wasn't for or about him—it was for and about the people he served.

Remember Larry? *"Gerren, it's 8:02. We hired you to do a job. I need you to go back to your desk and do that job."* Yeah, that Larry. He was my boss, and a man I looked up to. What if he'd set me on the fast track to my calling instead of ramming my motivation into the ditch of depression? I'd probably still be at that company today, working my tail off. And since my destiny was to coach, mentor, and teach, I see no reason why I couldn't have risen to CEO. Then I would have helped employees like young Gerren be all they could be, and grow the company to profitable levels beyond their wildest dreams.

I don't say any of this from a place of bitterness. Looking back, I truly am grateful for the turns my life took. What Larry said kicked me into entrepreneurial high gear, and the rest is history. Yet I can't help but imagine how many Larrys are out there who kill their employees' ambitions, hopes, and dreams at a critical moment in their careers. With over twenty million active businesses in North America, if we have just one Larry per company, that's twenty million calling-naysayers in the for-profit world alone. And that's just a guesstimate! We're not even talking churches, nonprofits, community organizations, and government agencies here. Chances are, you know who the Larry is in your organization. (We can assume it's not you!) If only we could reach the Larrys of the world, help *them* find their calling, and, in turn, help them help the people they supervise. Even as I say this, I must say that Larry is my guy. He was a cool supervisor; his words that day just sucked life out of me. So I use that experience as an example.

For now, all we can control is ourselves. What we do, what we say, and what we believe. That's it. But it's no small task. Giving people the opportunity to apply their knowledge and natural abilities, and also teaching them to make the most of it, has, I believe, eternal value. If you have employees, then of course they have a job to do. But in all my years of scaling my business, interviewing candidates, and training employees, I've learned one powerful lesson. One that every person can leverage, whether you're a pastor at a mega-church or manage one minimum-wage intern.

Here it is—*align your people well, and performance and profit follow*. Let's talk specifics. You can't align anyone if you don't know who you're dealing with or what they have to offer. Have you identified your people's strengths? Do you know where they fit in? Do you know what they naturally do well? How is that being played out on your team or in your organization? Should two or more employees actually switch roles based on their natural abilities and interests? Is that quiet, nurturing salesperson a better fit for the human resources job currently held by your assertive, outgoing employee, for example, and vice versa?

If you had your people working 80 percent of the time on what they love to do, how would that impact your business? Would they be happier? Would they be more efficient because of it? If your organization were a training ground, how much more would you get out of your people?

I helped Daisy align with her employer by connecting what she loves to do with what her supervisor needed her to do. I don't believe the old expression, "You can't teach an old dog new tricks." If someone finds something they really, really enjoy doing, they'll be open to learning it. With Daisy, we identified ways she could make her coworkers and customers alike feel special and valued . . . by learning computer skills. Win-win.

A while back, I saw one of my employees developing into a leader. She hadn't brought it up, but I saw in her someone who could keep people accountable. So I told her.

"I see you leading a team."

She smiled. I promoted her. Now she manages a team of eleven employees. I don't have to monitor her—or them—on site. Her team loves her attitude, her drive, her self-discipline. Everyone around her excels because she does. All it took was someone (me) to nudge her into the fast lane. Mentorship, not oversight, helps people find and pursue their callings.

You challenge people to be a better version of themselves that even *they* don't realize they can be.

Before that promotion, I had another employee who came complaining to me halfway through his shift.

"Hey, Gerren," my employee said. "I'm sick with a cold, and I'm having some problems at home right now. And to be honest, I'm really stressed about everything. I don't have the energy to work. I just want to go home. But I don't want to take time off."

"Yeah?" I said.

"Look, I know I've got a job to do. You guys are counting on me, but I don't know if I'm gonna make it. What do you think?"

I could tell he was hoping I'd go easy on him and just send him home. *Nope!* I saw a teachable moment instead.

"I'm with you. It's tough. Everybody gets sick. I get sick sometimes, and I still come to work. I do what I have to do. You mentioned that you're really stressed. So what's going on there? What's making you stressed?"

"I don't know. I like getting to talk to people here at Clean Slate. It feels good. So, I don't know, just personal things at home, my family."

"Right, right, I hear you," I said. "I've been there. Stress never helps you show up and perform. If you're stressed today and you feel like you can't perform, what are the chances you're going to feel like this again tomorrow? Even if your cold is gone? I think your stress is the real problem here. What if you gave yourself permission to let it go for a while? Just until the end of the day. If you focus on things that make you happy, you might be able to make it through and have an easier time dealing with your stress when you get home. What do you think?"

"So you're saying that maybe if I just focus on what I like doing, like talking to clients and our teammates, I might feel better?" He nodded to himself. "I guess you're right. I didn't think of that. I just didn't want to work today, but you're right. I probably won't want to work tomorrow either if I don't address what I'm dealing with at home."

"If you go home now, in the state that you're in, what will you do to solve what's stressing you?"

"I don't know. I hadn't thought of that just yet."

"If you didn't stay and work today, who do you think can perform the job the way you do when you're at your best and you're killing it?"

"I don't know. I know I do it really well, but someone else could probably . . . wait, no. It might not be the best job, but I'm sure someone else could do my job."

"Well, we need the best. Because what we've been getting from you has been the best, and that's what we've started to depend on. That's what our clients depend on," I said. "I'm okay with you taking a day off to settle your mind and so forth. What I need from you is to help me think through who we can bring onboard to perform like you."

"You know what? We don't need to go there. I can do it." My employee's posture straightened right up.

"Yeah?"

"Yeah, I think so. You're right. And you know what? Maybe if I just focus, the stress will lessen, and I'll feel better. I'll address the problem at home tonight. I've gotta get tougher on the inside so the next time I'm stressed, I won't crash like this."

"Is there anything that I can do to help you with that?"

"Just cut me a little slack if I'm a little slow today?"

"Okay, I can work with that. But you'll do your best with what you have, yeah?"

"Yes. Yes, I will."

"All right. I'll have one of your managers come around and just check behind you, and we'll give a little feedback. Not today. Tomorrow. Push through today if you can. Then call me at the end of the day. Tell me how you feel about what you did today when you're going home, and then we'll see if or how I can help."

"Man, that's what I love about you, Gerren. You're always there. You're so supportive. I really, really appreciate that."

"Any time."

Now, was that the perfect employer-employee conversation? No. Because there *is* no perfect way to mentor people. In tense or sensitive moments, you want your people to feel heard and cared for, and then they get to decide what they want to do. What could I have said? "If you leave today, I'm going to dock your pay. Don't even bother coming in tomorrow." Of course, I *could* have, but who the heck wants to hear that when they're stressed out? I take this same level of care with people who *aren't* my employees. Even if you're just here for an interview, I care about you. You have a story, you have a calling, and you have a reason why you're here. So why not care?

When you're nurturing the people around you, energy is more important than experience. I ask candidates and employees all of these questions because I want to know where their minds are. Are they dreaming about a future we can partner up on to help them reach? Or are they just in it for a paycheck? That's why I don't ask potential hires, "Can you tell me about a time when you accomplished a project?" I'm more about the flow. I've told several candidates, "If I feel good about what you're bringing to the space, we can work with you on the technical process of cleaning. That's minor. The energy you give off as a person, *that's* what's important to me."

Granted, my human resources department hates this line of questioning. It's not job-related or based on what showed up in the candidate's cover letter. "These questions are irrelevant," they tell me. "You're supposed to interview the person, not help them." But isn't that what good coaches, mentors, and teachers do? I'm all about bringing people on, helping them understand *why* I chose them, and setting them up for success. Show people you care, and you're probably going to throw them off a little. People aren't used to leaders who want to turn their followers into leaders, too. I once interviewed a young lady, whom I later hired. During our interview, she stopped me midsentence.

"Hold on, Mr. Sprauve. Why do you care? Why are you asking me all of these questions about my life and goals and everything? No one has ever asked me these questions before in an interview. Or even after I've gotten the job."

"I want to make sure we're a good fit," I said. "I want to ensure that we're good for you and that you're good for us. Does that make sense? I think that's only fair, don't you?

"Yeah," she said. "But nobody's ever asked me these kinds of questions. It's . . . different."

From there, once she came on board, she knew exactly *why* she was coming on board. Clean Slate wasn't just a job for her. It was about all the goals she needed to accomplish—and the fact that we were going to hold her accountable for accomplishing them. Now she comes into work every day with a purpose. She *knows* what she's working toward. Her job is more than a job—*it's her vehicle*. And over time—like every Clean Slate employee—she becomes a better version of herself.

Helping the people around you align with their destiny can be as simple as calling them out when they're *not* aligned with it. At Clean Slate, that means I tell the truth. And I help candidates tell their truth, too.

Another potential hire walked through my door and said with a straight face, "Hi. I want a job."

I happened to be at the front desk at the time, so I decided to turn our little meet-and-greet into an impromptu interview.

"No, you don't," I said. "You don't want a job." He was visibly confused. "Look, if you didn't *have* to work, you *wouldn't* work. What is it you *really* want to do?"

"What do you mean?" He raised his voice. "Of course I want a job." He lowered it again. The guy caught himself. He probably thought he was already disqualified.

"I hear you, but what do you *really* want to do in life? What is this job supposed to get you?"

The guy had a deadly serious look on his face. No white lies this time. "I want to take better care of my kids. That's what I want. That's why I want a job. I want to treat my son and my daughter better than my father treated me. It's important to me that I can provide for them." He looked dazed, like that was the very first time he'd verbalized any of this. "You know what I mean?"

"Yeah, I know what you mean," I said.

"It's just that—it's just that things are rough at home right now. I don't get to see my kids a whole lot. And I want them to be proud of me. Like I was never proud of my father. That's why I want a job. That's why I'll show up earlier than you ask me to, work harder than you ask me to, and stay later than you ask me to."

"How do you think we can help you do all that?"

"Well," he swallowed hard, eyes darting back and forth, "I guess I want to be in a place where I can learn, where I can feel respected. It's all about that mutual respect, right?"

"Right. Let me tell you a little about us. We're image consultants who happen to specialize in janitorial services. We improve our clients' office image, we keep everything nice and sanitary, and we do it all without getting in the way," I said. "Right now, we're looking for another full-time janitor. Do you think we're what you're looking for?"

"Yes, sir. Yes, I do."

"All right. Now, something else about Clean Slate," I said. "You said you want to learn in a respectful environment. If we hire you, we honor what you ask of us. In exchange, we ask you to honor what we ask of you. If there ever comes a point where one of us is falling short, we're going to have this conversation again. 'Are we still a good fit? Am I still doing for you what you need me to do for you?' Then we both share. It's back and forth."

"I can go along with that."

I nodded. "If it's working, then we keep working together. Until the time comes for you to go off to your next assignment."

"Right," he said. I offered him the job on the spot, and he accepted.

> **Pump Your Brakes**
> Leaders are supposed to grow people—then teach those people how to grow others. It's a cycle. Choose to focus on your responsibility, not on your title or rank.

Setting people up for success doesn't have to be difficult. All you have to do is set expectations high—yours *and* theirs. When I give my employees the tools they need to get the job done, and teach them the cleaning processes they need to know, I feel like I'm teaching them to drive their brand-new vehicle. I don't abandon them. I'm right there riding shotgun whenever they need some direction. But I don't ever turn off the GPS.

I tell my employees, "Go ahead and mess up a time or two. You're going to learn from it." If they do mess up, I speak to them with loving care. I say, "Okay, do you want to do better? What do *you* think better looks like?" I can tell them what *I* think is better, but I want *them* to grow, learn, and succeed, so I ask. That way I get to see exactly where they are and then take their "hands" (if they're willing) from there.

When you allow your people to fail *just enough* to learn, you build them. You get their confidence up. An employee gets to tell me—their CEO—what better looks like, and I design a process to turn their idea into a habit every employee has to learn. What does that communicate to my employee? *Wow, the owner of the company respects my opinion! How else can I make things more efficient around here?* And off they go to improve Clean Slate even further without me ever asking them to. Who needs micromanagement when you're surrounded by people whose callings align with yours?

At least for the time being. Why? Because more times than I can count, Clean Slate clients have hired away my employees. I'm not kidding. But you know what? *I'm glad*. My people possibly got a better opportunity at a better-paying job, and they *seized* it. They took the next road to their calling. After all, that's what Clean Slate is all about. If someone has the chance to be their very best at Clean Slate, and someone else notices and recognizes their talent, I say, "If we can't compete in that space, Go! But here's the deal. You'd better be a rock star for that company. Don't leave just to be subpar. If it's a step on your journey, be your very best."

I always check in with my former employees. We'll meet up for lunch and I'll ask them, "How are you doing? How can I help?" The same conversations I had when they were my employees are the same conversations I have with them now. I want them to be their best. I hope they all want to be their best, too.

It's important I tell you this. Some of my former employees who went on to work for other employers weren't all that happy over time. They thought they were moving on to a better opportunity, and in some cases they were. But one in particular shared with me that he wasn't happy. He said that he wasn't the rock star for his new employer like he was for us.

"I like working with my hands. I like walking into a place and doing something so that when I leave, I can look back and say, 'Wow, I did that!' I don't get that out of this new work. I go home, and I feel . . . unaccomplished. I get paid more, and I got benefits now. I'm just not happy."

What in the world? This guy's asking for his lower-paying job back? He had a family, so doing that probably wasn't in his best interest. But I could work with him.

"We're getting a lot of quote requests for floor refinishing and carpet cleaning. The pay is way better. I'm opening up a training program. You might try that. You would learn and absorb that information faster than anyone else we hired since you know how Clean Slate rolls. I could see you becoming one of our specialists for some projects."

Long story short, I was willing to help. You never know powerful or how potent a "toolbox" you have until you pour into the people around you and help them get closer to the things that energize them. To any leader worth their weight in Pine-Sol, that's a success story. Only a petty mind thinks a subordinate's success is their failure. If your heart is in the right place, you cannot help but create win-wins wherever you go. You may have to get a little creative, but the opportunities are *always* there.

Take one of my recent hires. The day Sanna started at Clean Slate, she took initiative—and I took notice. She came in early and stayed late. On her dime, on her time. She job-shadowed her supervisor and other long-time employees. Within weeks, I promoted *her* to supervisor. And now she's on the management fast track. I believe in giving people like Sanna the chance to do their thing, then getting out of the way. It's not abdication—it's a virtuous cycle. They add value to me and my business, I add value to them in the form of opportunities, promotions, and raises. The cycle just keeps going!

Who are the Sannas around you? Who works harder than they have to, longer than they get paid to, and lends a helping hand when no one asked them to? Talk to them. Ask, "Why do you do the things you do? What resonates with you most? Where do you believe we can help you do more of those things, and what do you think can happen as a result?" I know! That can be tough because, well, you're boss around here. You tell people what to do, right? Leaders are always the smartest ones in the room . . . in every category, right? Given the chance, some people, when nurtured in the things they are passionate about, will blow your mind by taking you and your business, your nonprofit, or your church further than you imagined possible.

Chances are if you overlook this opportunity, someone else will notice your superstar and win them away from you. Take my longtime mentor and good friend James. He teaches companies how to align diverse professionals and create a culture where everyone gets to pursue their strengths. After his hospital employer gave him an annual raise, he pushed for more.

"With the value I bring here and how passionate I am about culture, I know I've earned the opportunity for more."

"James. Come on," his direct supervisor told him. "Haven't we given you enough? Please don't rock the boat. Too much ambition is unwise."

James left that meeting angry—and emboldened. He took a meeting later that day with a recruiter.

"An international healthcare IT corporation sees your value," she said. "An offer is on the table."

That offer made James's jaw drop. It was *more* than he hoped for at the hospital! James accepted, excelled, and leaped his way up the organizational ladder. Within ten months, he traveled overseas to Dubai and India, training employees. He continues to be promoted, taking on more teams and being asked to deliver in critical areas.

The lesson to take away from James? Don't stifle ambition. Don't be threatened by an employee, student, or team member who shows greater promise than even *you*. The best leaders train leaders they themselves can one day follow.

I'm not saying you should hand the reins of your organization to a young up-and-comer. Just give them a chance to prove themselves even if they aren't qualified on paper or don't fit your idea of the right candidate. People tend to surprise you.

Take Al, for example, a long-time Clean Slate employee. Al's work ethic, attention to detail, and ability to train his coworkers came from years of working in the tourism industry.

"When I look back at what I was doing, I realized how confident I was in the team members," Al said to me one day. "All I had to do was say, 'That's your storeroom, so start packing the supplies we need.' These workers didn't need any supervision, because the contracting company had already trained them. No on-the-job training required, no cleaning up messes they made while learning. They already know what temperature the fridge should be, what temperature the freezer should be, and so on. It made my job so easy."

"So you could just look at something, at anything, and think, 'Hey, it should be *this* way'?" I asked.

"That's right, chief."

"Huh." I nodded. "You know, I've had some extra administrative work on my plate that needs to get done. Like, done yesterday. You've said before you're not a computer guy, but do you have any idea how I could get some reports done?"

"What kind of reports?"

"Who are we hiring, who are we training, how are our supervisors doing, the whole nine."

"I can take care of those for you. No problem."

"Really?"

"Yeah, chief. I'll have 'em to you within two days."

I admit I was skeptical. Al was the last guy I knew to give up his flip phone. How easy to read would these reports be? But when someone offers to help, you let them prove you wrong. And wrong I was.

Two days later, I pulled up an email from Al as I walked into a job site. The attached reports looked beautiful. Crisp, clean layout. All the details I asked for plus some I'd forgotten about.

"Yo, Al! You did all this?" I called across the parking lot. Al headed in to supervise the evening crew.

"So you got what you wanted?" he said when we got closer.

"These reports are good stuff! I thought you said you hated computers."

"I do. Let me tell you what happened. I just picked up my phone, called a few ladies I knew who were looking for extra work and were comfortable delivering on this. I trusted them and told them what we needed. They made it happen. I got to free up my time and make money while I was sleeping."

"Feels good, doesn't it?"

"Yeah, chief."

"Listen, I am gonna need more reports like these. More tasks done like *that*." I snapped my fingers. "Is that something you'd consider doing long term? Kinda like a side hustle. Again, separate from Clean Slate."

Al beamed ear to ear. We shook hands, and from that moment on, I was the first official client of Al's virtual assistant company. I see him growing his company right alongside ours and working closely with other organizations helping them grow, too. (If that's what he wants to do.) That's what a fast-tracked calling is all about.

If there's anything I've taught you in this book, it's that cleaning—like any line of work—is just a vehicle. Where you (and your employees or students) are is *not* the end goal. For now, make the most of it. Help your people read the map so they know what their calling is. Recalculate where they're at so they know how close to their goals they already are, right here and now in your organization. Then get in the car with them and encourage them to drive that vehicle forward for everything it's worth. Help them shore up their strengths and patch up their weaknesses. Make sure they know to carpool with colleagues or peers with similar or complementary callings. And when they've arrived, teach them to celebrate—and share everything they learned with the next person.

If everyone did that, then maybe—just maybe—we'd have a world where every single person ends up in the right career, leaders turn followers into success stories, and Ponche Kuba releases a nonalcoholic option.

You with me?

Key Point

When we help people find who they are and nurture them, they may say thank you and stick around to help you, too. Or you may have to let them go to pursue their calling while you find the right next person. It's a tough decision, but you don't want to force them to stay. Allow people to think how they can help others with their strengths. How much better would people be if they did what they were supposed to do?

Action Steps

1. As a leader, remember that it's not about you. Leaders grow others, no matter what the position is. Your responsibility is to serve those around

you, including those who look up to you or work for you.

2. Get curious about the people below you. Create opportunities to let your team work on anything they want. Give your people a brief window of time in the week to do whatever they want to do. Let them brainstorm and follow their ideas.

- For example, create an anonymous online form for your employees or students to share their ideas to improve the business or class experience. Let everyone speak! Then when you pick an idea to run with, you call out and give credit to the person who is now pursuing their calling right where they are—contributing in a way they never thought about before.

3. Be vulnerable with your team. Share with people your mistakes. Let them see themselves in your journey. Many people look at their jobs as a dead end.

4. Remind everyone that they're working there for a reason.

- "What can you learn from this job?"

- "What can you take from this experience that will serve you elsewhere?"

- "What do you need to get better at while you're here?"

Acknowledgments

I've stayed in the game because I have an awesome group of people around me. To my siblings, I love you all. My Groupme Orlando Family, thank you for supporting and loving me. To my daughters, Madison and Morgan, Daddy will always love you. To my friends who encouraged my growth, thank you. Jamara Wilson, who came into my world right on time, thank you. To my past and current team members, thank you for going on your journey. To Zynia Spencer, thank you for that nudge years ago to do this.

What's Next?

www.GerrenSprauve.com/Assessment

What is your calling? How do you know if what you are doing in life is what you *should* be doing? Is your calling closer than you think? This free assessment helps you get clarity on where you are supposed to be in your career, in your ministry, and in your life.

www.GerrenSprauve.com/Assessment

www.ingramcontent.com/pod-product-compliance
Lightning Source LLC
Chambersburg PA
CBHW021818170526
45157CB00007B/2629